Reconciling the Solitudes

Essays on Canadian Federalism and Nationalism

Charles Taylor

Edited by Guy Laforest

McGill-Queen's University Press
Montreal & Kingston • London • Buffalo

© Charles Taylor
ISBN 0-7735-1105-9 (cloth)
ISBN 0-7735-1110-5 (paper)

Legal deposit second quarter 1993
Bibliothèque nationale du Québec
Printed in Canada on acid-free paper

Publication has also been supported
by the Canada Council
through its block grant program.

Canadian Cataloguing in Publication Data

Taylor, Charles, 1931–

Reconciling the solitudes: essays on
Canadian federalism and nationalism
ISBN 0-7735-1105-9 (bound)
ISBN 0-7735-1110-5 (pbk.)
1. Canada – Politics and government – 1963–1984.
2. Canada – Politics and government – 1984–.
3. Canada – English-French relations. 4. Federal
government – Canada. 5. Nationalism – Canada.
I. Title.

FC164.T39 1993   971.064   C93-090173-8
F1026.6.T39 1993

Typeset in Palatino 10/12
by Caractéra production graphique inc.,
Quebec City

Contents

Preface

This book owes its origins to Guy Laforest. It was he who suggested that these articles and essays – written at different times and for various purposes – might enhance one another and form a coherent whole.

In all likelihood he will be proved correct, for these pieces do indeed have the same themes and preoccupations: national identity, the bases of citizenship in a modern democracy, and the possibility of a real agreement between Quebec and the various regions and societies that form this unstable and constantly evolving amalgamation that we call Canada.

One too easily falls prey to the habit of speaking separately to the audiences who define themselves as distinct. Since each of these audiences has its own perspective, its own key terms, and its own premises; the starting point of the discourse is different in each case. In former times, Canadian politicians were often accused of saying different things in Quebec than they said in English Canada. In fact, it is almost impossible not to do so, even when there is not the slightest intention of trickery. I do not pretend that our politicians were never dishonest. Far from it. But I do maintain that a rigorously honest discourse cannot be identical in both contexts.

Taking all this into consideration, I agreed that it could be illuminating to bring together a selection of papers addressed to Quebec and non-Quebec audiences, and to place them side by side. By doing so, we might bring out something important and commentators who have been intimately or even peripherally involved in the recent constitutional negotiations in Canada.

On the topic of democracy, Taylor cautions those who swear by charters of rights and the safeguards they offer citizens. He reminds them that the vogue for charters can mean a withering away of political life, an estrangement of citizens from their public institutions in modern societies. Taylor's warnings come at a time when the Charter of Rights and Freedoms of 1982 is on its way to becoming the real founding myth of the Canadian political community. As well, Taylor enriches our understanding of nationalism, both in its theoretical aspects and in its incarnations within Canadian and Quebec society. He does not deify nationalism, any more than he holds it up to public obloquy. On this question, as on many others, the paths followed by his thought are those of measure, of the median way between extremes in accordance with the parameters of Aristotelian ethics. According to Taylor, nationalism emerges in the modern age as a legitimate form of identification; so instead of trying to impose on people the vision of a single Canadian national identity, our constitutional negotiators ought first to attempt to understand the various feelings of national belonging, recognizing that they are different in Chicoutimi from what they are in Swift Current, Toronto, or Whitehorse.

In this book, Charles Taylor also proposes a finely shaded reading of liberalism and the concept of justice associated with it. Taking inspiration from Aristotle, the much-missed political scientist Donald Smiley claimed in one of his last publications that justice consists of treating equals equally, and unequals unequally.[1] The crisis shaking our country is not made any simpler by the multiform face of the aspiration to equality – an aspiration of individuals as citizens of one and the same political system; of language groups; and of groups representing people of diverse cultural backgrounds, societies, nations, and peoples. In short, everybody aspires to equality and nobody wants to be pushed aside or subjected to any form of discrimination. Liberalism, according to Taylor, can embrace both the rights of individuals and the rights of the many communities to which they belong, without equity being synonymous with symmetry. Granting distinct treatment to a minority language group – in Quebec – or to aboriginal peoples is not incompatible with the liberal tradition.

A democracy centred more around citizen participation, a political system open to national pluralism, and a liberalism able to balance the rights of citizens with those of communities – all of this will become possible in Canada only if we succeed in renewing our federal system from top to bottom. Charles Taylor outlines a genuine political philosophy of renewed federalism for the medium and longer term. This renewed federalism involves an acknowledgment of diversity and its need for self-expression in common political institutions without renouncing the guarantees that liberalism affords individuals. Because the problem of managing cultural and national pluralism is not about to disappear from our horizon, this collection of Charles Taylor's contributions will withstand the passage of time. Their relevance will not be exhausted by the outcome of the Canada-Quebec crisis.

It was, however, necessary for these texts to be published in the context of our constitutional saga, for their author is not unaware of the short-term imperatives, those of the current situation. To those people who dwell only on the instrumental dimensions of the issue, who compute the number and importance of the powers transferred to the provinces, the economic barriers reduced, the overlappings eliminated in relations between governments – to these critics, Taylor cites the fundamental importance of the symbols that define a political community's identity, and the recognition that societies, peoples, and nations bestow – or refuse to bestow – on themselves. What does it mean when partners in a federation agree to regard Quebec as a distinct society, to grant an inherent right of self-government to aboriginal peoples, or choose to define Canada as a multinational federation rather than presenting it as a bilingual and multicultural nation-state? According to Taylor, questions of this type are the most urgent ones facing Canada. The different actors involved ought to devote their best efforts to trying to answer these questions. And whatever happens, whether the country remains intact or breaks up, Quebec and Canada (from which Quebec would on the second hypothesis be severed) will remain complex societies in which calls for recognition will arise from a good number of distinct, particular communities.

Charles Taylor's writings on federalism and nationalism in Canada should interest two other audiences, the most limited and the broadest of those mentioned in this introduction. Some years ago, the American thinker Benjamin Barber underlined the fact that in the Western tradition very few philosophers of high calibre had dared to dirty their hands in the partisan politics of their country. The exceptions to the rule, according to Barber, were people such as Edmund Burke and Charles Taylor.[2] In 1992 the latter received the Canada Council's Molson Prize, awarded to a scholar who has worked with distinction in the area of the humanities and social sciences. Charles Taylor was honoured for the quality of his work in a remarkable range of areas: the philosophy of psychology and language, the epistemology of the human sciences, the study of German thought from the seventeenth century to the present, the interpretation of modern civilization, and the development of an original political philosophy. He has also just received Quebec's highest distinction for a career in the human and social sciences, the Léon-Gérin Award. In this book on Canadian and Quebec politics, specialists in these various disciplines who are interested in Taylor's work will discover the way that he is rooted in his situation and the source that inspired several of his theoretical adventures. Taylor has never made any mystery of this, as is shown by the following excerpt from a paper he delivered in Montreal in the fall of 1988 during a conference commemorating the twentieth anniversary of André Laurendeau's death:

When I was a student in Europe, in a foreign country therefore, I felt a very strong affinity with Herder, the eighteenth-century German philosopher and one of the founders of modern nationalist thinking. Herder devoted much thought to language, the difference between languages, and the distortion in the thinking of a given language group when a language claims to be superior and better able to express universality, and when it therefore represses other languages. At the time, that language was French, which was invading the German intellectual world and was marginalizing German ... I was able to understand him from the situation I had experienced outside school, outside university, and I was able to engage with his thought, internalize it, and (I hope) make something interesting out of it.[3]

Specialists in Charles Taylor's work know that he studied history at McGill and philosophy at Oxford before returning to settle in

Montreal in the early 1960s. However, they may not know that his political thought was nurtured by long years of activism in social democratic organizations in England and Canada. From 1961 to 1971, Taylor set his shoulder to the wheel to help the New Democratic Party (NDP) establish itself in Quebec. In this endeavour, he took over from F.R. Scott, the valiant law professor from McGill University who devoted the greater part of his time in that period to the renowned Royal Commission on Bilingualism and Biculturalism. Charles Taylor was defeated four times during the federal elections that took place in Canada between 1962 and 1968. He was Pierre Elliott Trudeau's opponent in the riding of Mount Royal during the 1965 ballot, two years after having benefited from the support of this friend and university colleague. It is also worth noting that Taylor was one of the group that succeeded the Pelletier and Trudeau generation in running the magazine *Cité libre*. Throughout these years, he was also an assiduous contributor to *Canadian Dimension*, the intellectual magazine of the English-Canadian left. From 1966 to 1971, he worked as federal vice-president of the NDP, but he considerably cut back his militant activities after the 1971 NDP conference at which Tommy Douglas was replaced as party leader by David Lewis. From then on, Taylor devoted all of his time and effort to consolidating his philosophical work.

After having worked for a decade at fostering greater understanding between Québécois and English-speaking Canadians, and after having tried to find a synthesis of both sides' visions of federalism, Taylor sought to make explicit the epistemological and theoretical foundations of his political action. This induced him to take long and fruitful detours in the philosophy of the social sciences through the incomparably difficult and rigorous thought that is Hegel's. His efforts were crowned with success in 1975 with the publication of a voluminous, critically acclaimed work on the thought of that German philosopher. Taylor returned to Oxford between 1976 and 1979 to take up the Chichele chair of social and political theory, one of the most prestigious positions in the entire Anglo-American academic world.

He returned to Montreal in the fall of 1979 to take part in the referendum campaign that was shaping up. Once again, he had the impression that his finely shaded and complex vision of federalism was squeezed between the more extreme positions of the Trudeaus and Lévesques. During the 1980s, Taylor pursued his international philosophy career with great determination, keeping Montreal and McGill University as home base. Meanwhile, the difficulties and political fate of Canada and Quebec continued to preoccupy him greatly. It will be seen in this book that he studied in turn the consequences for Canadian political culture of the adoption of a Charter of Rights and Freedoms, as well as the dangers for Quebec society of the exhaustion and delegitimization of public institutions.

After the failure of the Meech Lake Accord in 1990, Charles Taylor was one of the experts consulted by the parliamentary commission set up to determine the constitutional and political future of Quebec. His brief to the Bélanger-Campeau Commission makes up one of the chapters of this book. If German thinkers such as Herder and Hegel provided Taylor with some of the intuitions that guided his thought, it is Aristotle's wisdom that one encounters in his writings on Canada and Quebec. Abstract philosophy cannot impose a theoretical model of a system on a political community. The best system is always the one that takes into account the particular circumstances in which the citizens of a country live. Taylor has worked hard to convince his compatriots to subscribe to his vision of the best system for Canada and Quebec. When his suggestions have not been accepted, he has not remained silent. Following Aristotle's example, he has set out to find approaches and measures that could bring about stability and momentum in the Canadian political system even when he found it imperfect. It will immediately be noticed that his suggestions were sometimes daring and radical. Whatever happens on the Canadian political scene in the near future, no overall interpretation of Charles Taylor's philosophical work will be able to avoid a study of its roots in the dilemmas of the society to which he belongs.

If those who favour national pluralism and the acceptance of the differences between societies give in, and if the Canada-Quebec partnership ends in failure, Charles Taylor will have lost one of the most important political fights of his life. The texts brought together here show that things could have happened otherwise and that they still can happen otherwise if the voices of moderation are heard. History will soon decide.

The Canadian experience is fraught with meaning for the world. This book's ultimate audience is outside our country, among those who have to ponder the ways forward available to complex societies that are pervaded by the diversity of origins and the pluralism of forms of belonging. In 1989, the very year in which the fall of the Berlin Wall prefigured the upheavals lying in store for our world, Charles Taylor published a magnum opus with Harvard University Press: *Sources of the Self: The Making of the Modern Identity.*[4] Like Isaiah Berlin (who was Taylor's teacher at Oxford), Taylor believes that there are several ways of living in the modern age and that the spirit of liberal democracy does not require individuals and peoples to renounce their identity. At best, the Canadian political experience consists of a long and patient effort to bring the parameters of such thinking into being in the institutions of a federation. The value of this thinking for the human adventure after the upheavals of 1989 is not tied to the ultimate fortune of the Canadian experience.

Guy Laforest

Notes

1 Donald Smiley, "Language Policies in the Canadian Political Community," in *Etre contemporain: Mélanges en l'honneur de Gérard Bergeron*, ed. J.W. Lapierre, V. Lemieux, and J. Zylberberg (Sillery: Les Presses de l'Université du Québec, 1992), 284.
2 Benjamin Barber, *The Conquest of Politics: Liberal Philosophy in Democratic Times* (Princeton: Princeton University Press, 1988), 8.
3 Charles Taylor, "La Tradition d'une situation," in *Penser l'éducation: Nouveaux dialogues avec André Laurendeau*, ed. Nadine Pirotte (Montréal: Boréal, 1989), 87–8.
4 Charles Taylor, *Sources of the Self: The Making of the Modern Identity* (Cambridge, Mass.: Harvard University Press, 1989).

My thanks to Jean-François Nadeau for preparing the index.

G.L.

Reconciling the Solitudes

CHAPTER ONE

Nationalism and the Political Intelligentsia: A Case Study

This chapter was published, in its original form, in the *Queen's Quarterly* in 1965. In it the author addressed an incredulous English-Canadian audience (which believed that French-Canadian nationalism would disappear with *Duplessisme*) in order to explain the rise of the new nationalism that was associated with efforts towards the liberal modernization of Quebec society. The analysis deals mainly with the role of the renewed, better-educated, more diversified intelligentsia, which was concentrated mostly in Montreal. Taylor contended that French-Canadian and Quebec élites wanted reforms that would enable them to become genuinely responsible for their society and rival the rest of America on all fronts in the modern age. He pointed out that the political dimension of the reforms being considered – in other words, the temptation of sovereignty – differentiated this project from that of the traditional left, whose principal aim is the construction of the welfare state. Since this text was written more than a quarter of a century ago, the wording has been revised for this collection, the present tense systematically being replaced by the past tense.

IN THE EARLY 1960S, A WAVE OF NATIONALISM swept French Quebec, but unlike previous waves this one was heard and felt far beyond its frontiers. In part this was because of the acts of the extreme terrorist wing of the nationalist movement, which were widely reported, in the way these acts always are, in both the

Taken from *Queen's Quarterly* 72 (Spring 1965).

United States and Europe. But in part the wider press that this wave of nationalism attracted was due to an intrinsic difference that marked it off from previous waves, a difference both of style and of goal.

The difference was symbolized if not adequately represented by the demand of the most far-reaching groups for independence for Quebec. Although at the time this was by no means a majority demand among French Canadians, or even among the French-Canadian intelligentsia, it was adequate as a symbol, since the demands of modern nationalism have all gone in this direction, even though they have not gone quite as far; that is, they tend to the goal of a French Canada assuming control over its destiny via the provincial government of Quebec, which will in the process have arrogated greater powers to itself, largely at the expense of the federal government of Canada. Between separatists and non-separatist nationalists there is very often only a difference of degree.

Separatism had existed in the past in French Canada, though it was probably never as powerful before; but since its overt strength was not very powerful in the early 1960s, this was not the real difference. The difference was that separatism had never previously been the central issue, never the nodal point around which all strands of nationalism were distributed, the issue with which they were all obsessed. Separatism became this issue, I would maintain, not because of its political force but because of what I have called above its symbolic value, for it symbolized a French Canada which, after a couple of centuries of enforced incubation, was ready to take control once more of its own history.

This is what marked the new nationalism and distinguished it from the dominant stream in the tradition of French-Canadian nationalism. I would like to emphasize the words "dominant stream" because nothing is new under the sun, least of all in French Canada, and the new form of nationalism had its fore-runners and antecedents all the way through French-Canadian history. But it was never the dominant form of nationalism before, and this is what was decisively new. The previous nationalist tradition made recurrent demands for autonomy – which, after all, is only quantitatively different from independence – but a more profound difference underlay this.

The old nationalism was defensive; it was oriented around the defence of a way of life that was held already to exist but was in danger of being, if not submerged, at least undermined by the more robust North American culture alongside which it lived. It was meant to defend a civilization based on a set of values, mainly the religious values of a certain interpretation of Roman Catholicism and the linguistic values of the ancestral language. It was feared that these values would ultimately lose out to the North American values of material progress, of wider communication, of the cult of achievement. But, of course, the best way for this form of nationalism to achieve its goals would have been to isolate French Canada totally from the surrounding environment. And if we go back not even as much as a century, we can find examples of this – for instance, the colonization movement of the late nineteenth century which attempted to channel the excess rural population of French Canada towards the agricultural frontier and away from the large cities, away from the centres of industrialization, and away from the United States, which received substantial Quebec emigration in this period. Only in this way, its proponents felt, could the traditional French-Canadian way of life, based on the village parish, survive.

Of course this attempt failed, for both figuratively and literally the ground was too stony and infertile, but in other forms the attempt to insulate French Canada continued. In the immediate postwar years and until 1960, Quebec was governed by a regime under Maurice Duplessis, whose basic goal (to the extent that we can discern one, in the shifting sands of opportunism) seems to have been to preside over the development of the province principally by the exploitation of its natural resources, without allowing French Canada to develop the form of social structure and outlook that seemed inevitably to go along with twentieth-century affluence. Needless to say, these attempts also failed.

The basis of the new nationalism, on the other hand, was not the defence of anything existing; it was the creation of something new. Its aim was not to defend the traditional way of life but to build a modern French society on this continent. In its pure form, practically the only value it had in common with the old was the French language itself. The rest of what has been defined as the French-Canadian tradition was seen in a very negative light. The modern nationalists were often anticlerical, if not unbelievers, and in any case the traditional conception of Catholicism in this society was anathema to them. Among certain of the younger people, particularly the students, there seemed also to be a powerful allergy to the traditional conception of a lettered culture, the culture that was handed down in the *collège classique* and supposedly stemmed from the classical period of French literature, whose literary values were preserved in a somewhat stiff, provincial style. One of the most important developments on the intellectual and artistic scenes in French Canada in the early 1960s was the founding of the highly successful, revolutionary, socialist, and nationalist review, *Parti pris*. This review reflected the rejection by many young writers of the traditional conception of an educated man and a lettered culture, which the *collège classique* had made dominant in French Canada. Indeed, rejection is too soft a word here; the contemplation of the traditional culture seemed to provoke paroxysms of frenzied iconoclasm in many of the educated youth. One finds the same determined if not deliberate use of obscenity as a destructive weapon among these writers as one finds in some writers of the beat generation.

Independence could be the symbol even if not always the actual goal of the new nationalism because, in the era of decolonization, it represented the awakening of underdeveloped societies that were determined to take control of their own history and in doing so to wrest it from both foreign domination and the dead hand of millennial tradition. It represented the kind of nationalism that could affirm the nation over and against the colonial power while at the same time denying in the name of a rejuvenated future what the nation actually was, in large part.

Outsiders, and particularly English Canadians, were very much taken by surprise by these developments. Having identified nationalism for so long with the tradition-minded defensive form of thought with which it was formerly connected, they expected to see it wither away once this form of thought came under critical fire. The rebirth of nationalism from its own ashes appeared to them diabolically miraculous, but in trying to explain why this happened we may come closer to an understanding of nationalism as a political phenomenon in the modern world.

THE NEW INTELLIGENTSIA

The rise of the new form of nationalism was, I maintain, largely the result of a change in the class of French Canada that could be designated by the word "intelligentsia." To the extent that it was not directly due to the rise of the new intelligentsia, it can be traced to the social and economic developments that brought about the rise of this new group. The use of the word "intelligentsia" here may need some justification. We are used to it in connection with Russia in the nineteenth century, or the societies of Eastern Europe, as a term designating a class of people who had achieved a certain educational standard. This is the way I want to use it here, taking *collège classique* and the university as the criteria. But although there is in all advanced countries a group of people who have taken a university degree, we cannot say that the term "intelligentsia" can be given a use everywhere, for it implies also that there is a gulf between these people and the rest of the population, as indeed there was in nineteenth-century Russia. In Anglo-Saxon countries, on the other hand, with universal education having been the rule for something up to a century, the lines of demarcation between the people of different educational levels has become more and more blurred; there is a continuum rather than a sharp break. As a result, the way of life does not differ sharply between those at different levels, so a term like "intelligentsia" seems to have no meaning. The French Canada of the 1960s was hardly in the same plight as nineteenth-century Russia, and indeed the spread of education and rising living standards was gradually carrying it towards the North American norm; but there had traditionally been a gap between the educated classes and the rest of the population which legitimates the use of the term "intelligentsia" in this context.

Not only was the class of the more educated more distant from the rest of the society, it was also more important; this was because of the very special situation of French Canada. Just as the clergy assumed a very important role because of the leadership function that they were called on to take up after the Conquest, so in a society oriented to the need of cultural resistance and cultural survival did the professional classes have a special importance and a special prestige; their importance was enhanced by the high degree of foreign ownership of Quebec industry and commerce, for this robbed French-Canadian society of a business power élite; the power élite was a foreign one, made up of English Canadians or Americans. In French-speaking society, therefore, the summit was the professional classes.

When one looks at the role the intelligentsia played here, it is not surprising that they would take the lead in any nationalist movement. Even if we had not already been accustomed in observing nationalist movements abroad to find the educated middle classes in the forefront, we could have predicted this of Quebec. The results of the survey carried out in 1963 by the Groupe de recherche sociale of Montreal, which I shall return to below, confirm this view. The fact that nationalism was mainly a passion of the intelligentsia can also be seen if we look at the newspapers. Those exclusively directed to this class, such as Montreal's *Le Devoir*, were almost totally absorbed by the national question. Those mainly directed to a popular audience, such as the weekly *La Patrie* and, even more, the daily *Montréal matin*, were much less so, although both contained a certain dose of nationalist reporting and editorializing.

We can therefore hope to find at least part of the explanation for the change in the style of goals of nationalism by looking at the changes in the French-Canadian intelligentsia. The older intelligentsia covered a narrower range – basically the professional classes of lawyers, doctors, notaries, and of course (occupying a rather peculiar position) the clergy. The class was spread more evenly across the province, and social mobility was not very great, except of course as concerned the clergy, to which the sons of the poor regularly gained access if they had a vocation. The lay professions were, however, considerably harder to enter for those whose parents were not rich enough to send them to the *collège classique*.

The new intelligentsia were notably different. First of all, they were more numerous relative to the population; secondly, they were distributed in a much wider range of jobs. Many more young French Canadians were entering business, both on their own, in small or middle-sized firms, and in large international corporations. Many were employed in the growing communications industries, in the expanding public bureaucracies, and in other professions (for instance, as architects or engineers). We can take the engineering profession as an example of the expansion of the French-Canadian professional middle classes into a new field. In the 1940–41 academic session, the Ecole Polytechnique de Montréal gave only 30 diplomas; in the academic session of 1960–61 it gave 232 diplomas. In 1963 the Corporation of Professional Engineers of Quebec had a membership that was about 50 per cent French-speaking. Thirty years earlier, there was hardly a handful of French engineers in the province.

Thirdly, a higher proportion of the new intelligentsia were in Montreal – as was inevitable, considering the role of the city in the entire development, industrialization, and urbanization of Quebec that had brought the new intelligentsia into being. In 1941, Montreal had a population of a little over 1 million in a province of not much more than 4 million. By 1961, its population was more than 2 million in a province of 5.5 million. Its growth therefore accounted for the greater part of the population growth in the province in the intervening twenty years. This concentration in the metropolis, with its cosmopolitan atmosphere and a population that was almost 40 per cent non–French Canadian, put the greater part of the new intelligentsia in an atmosphere which most of its predecessors did not breathe. We shall see below the results of this close contact with English Canada. Fourthly, the new intelligentsia were the product of widespread mobility. They were recruited from a much wider social spectrum than the old, and this democratization was increasing. It was estimated, for instance, that 31 per cent of the students at the University of Montreal in 1961 were from working-class families, and another 11 per cent from peasant families.

These developments, together with the underlying economic growth that brought them about, made the old form of nationalism impossible. The development of a modern economy, the concentration of the population in large urban areas, particularly where they were in maximum contact with the rest of North American civilization, no longer permitted the isolation of French-Canadian society, which was the goal that in one form or another the old form of nationalism had been bound to seek. As was mentioned above, the final attempt under the government of Maurice

Duplessis ultimately broke down. The attempt was to give the province the material benefits of economic progress without allowing it to develop into the type of modern society most industrialized countries already had. This could not possibly succeed; at least, it could not succeed without destroying democracy, which fortunately the context of a federal Canada would never permit a Quebec leader to do. In time, therefore, the authoritarian pattern of traditional society was destroyed by mass education, by the development of mass democratic organizations such as trade unions and credit unions, and by the spread of state television to all corners of the land. With the death of Duplessis in 1959, his successor tried to take a new course; and when he, too, prematurely died, the regime itself crumbled.

The old form of nationalism was therefore impossible to realize, but it was also less and less popular among the new intelligentsia, for obvious reasons. This new intelligentsia had too much of a stake in the order of an industrialized – or, at least, industrializing – modern economy of Quebec. One cannot be an engineer or a television producer or businessman and remain fully committed to the re-creation of pre-industrial modes of life. The development of a new structure in the intelligentsia of French Quebec therefore set a term to traditional nationalism. But why dit it create a nationalism of a new form?

THE NEW NATIONALISM

In fact, the very process of urbanization and the development of a modern economy in Quebec, which did more than anything else to undermine the older defensive form of nationalism, was what created the pressures that lay behind the new form of nationalism. More and more French Canadians had been working cheek by jowl with English Canadians in a modern advanced economy in large corporations. In short, they were becoming less and less isolated from the English Canadians and increasingly were being forced to operate with them in the scope of the same institutions and by the same set of rules. But granted the history of economic development in Quebec, and the ownership of the bigger part of Quebec industry by those who were not French Canadian, these rules were usually made by English-speaking people, and one of the rules was generally that things be done in English. French Canadians in this situation were bound to be at a certain disadvantage; they were in some ways in the same position as immigrants are on this Anglo-Saxon continent; that is, as people who have to conform to another way of life, who have to learn a new language and forget their own background in order to succeed. But French Canadians are not and do not see themselves as being in the same historical position as immigrants. They have no intention of losing their language; they have no intention of seeing their children grow up in another language group. On the contrary, they intend to survive, and therefore the position of the immigrant is fundamentally intolerable for them – not only in Canada, which is supposed to be their country, but particularly in the province of Quebec, where they are in a majority.

Cases of conscious discrimination may have been few, but there was inevitable unconscious discrimination, since the ways in which French employees expressed themselves were often little understood by an English-Canadian superior. The predicament was therefore harmful or thought to be harmful to French Canadians' chances for promotion. And since the entering of a modern economy brought with it the ambition to succeed and the normal expectations of rising, it could be a dramatic experience for those who, on entering this particular slot of twentieth-century society, found or felt that they found the avenues closed to them because of a fact about themselves which their whole background had trained them never to give up in any circumstances.

This factor of expectations played a very important role. In order to see the importance of the position of the French Canadian in large English-speaking enterprises as a generator of nationalist tension, we must not only look to people who were themselves passed over for jobs or were in direct immediate line for a promotion they did not get. Very often, nationalist fervour was more evident among the younger people who were just entering the economy, or even among students who had not yet entered it. So we have to look not just at where these people were at that time but at how far they expected to get and how far they felt it was normal to expect to get.

Even where the chances for promotion and the making of a career were not affected, French Canadians inevitably felt the strain of operating in another language throughout their working lives, a strain which immigrants are quite accustomed to and accept as part of the terms of their entry into another society. This selfsame strain was seen by many French Canadians as a systematic and long-drawn-out insult to the original inhabitants of the country, who consider that it is the employer, rather than themselves, who is the immigrant. The position was all the more difficult for those who had made their way up from more humble origins. It was a fact in French-Canadian society – and had been since the Conquest – that the children of the upper income brackets were given the kind of training that fitted them to operate with comparative ease in an Anglo-Saxon environment. They were taught good English at an early age, given the chance to travel, given a sense of their own cultural superiority in the *collège classique*, along with the necessary social graces to maintain this sense, both in their own eyes and very often in the eyes of their English-Canadian interlocutors. Totally different was the position of someone born in the rural areas, in a working-class or peasant family, who had very little opportunity to learn English up to the standard required, and even less experience of operating in another world than his own.

The inevitable demand that arose that French Canadians be permitted to operate in their own language in the economy of Quebec ran up against the fact that this economy had for so long been dominated by those who were not French Canadian and who saw no reason to operate differently than they did in Ontario, Minnesota, or California, and not much reason to treat French-Canadian personnel differently from Poles or Italians. When the number of French Canadians in this position was relatively small and they felt therefore that their bargaining power was weak (not only because they were few but because they were, generally speaking, not very well qualified), the fact that the economic life of the province was run by the English did not arouse much protest. But those days have gone forever. By the early 1960s, not only was the bargaining power of the French professional classes greater than it had been in the past, but many of them had discovered that nationalist agitation in itself increased this bargaining power; for example, the noise made around the separatist movement made English Canadians more ready to make concessions in matters such as bilingualism and the use of French.

Nevertheless, it would be a mistake to give too rationalist and utilitarian a model of explanation to the rise and continuance of French-Canadian nationalism. The English dominance in Quebec was not just ultimately a matter of jobs; it hurt in a more subtle way, a way that brings us to the roots of nationalist sentiment. Its definition, although extremely difficult, is very important for our understanding of this sentiment. This analysis raises of course the problem of identity, the problem of how individuals or members of a group see themselves – or, as we say, what they identify themselves as. Educated French Canadians, like their counterparts anywhere else in North America, have to deal with people not only from their own circle, not only from their own part of the country, but from all kinds of backgrounds and from everywhere. Like everyone else, they expect a normal degree of recognition from those they deal with; and like everyone else, they hope that they compare well with these people in their own eyes.

To compare oneself with anyone else always raises the problem of identity. How does one differ from one's interlocutor? In the name of what does one ask him to respect one? This is the question that raises a problem in French Canada. There are, roughly speaking, two possible answers. One is to say, "My identity is as a North American on the same footing as all the others." But, as North Americans, French Canadians are in a rather absurd position. They do not belong to the dominant North American culture; nor are they, like immigrants, people who fail to belong to that culture only provisionally and are destined to assimilate to it or see their children assimilate to it in time. On the contrary, they intend to remain separate, and they intend that their children remain separate. So this identification really does not work. French Canadians therefore identify themselves over and against the North American norm as something different. But this difference immediately excites comparison, and the comparison shows that in certain crucial respects – which are very important in the context of North American civilization, in the fields of economic achievement and social progress and democratic mores – French Canada compares ill with the North American norm.

The problem is that the members of the new intelligentsia of the 1960s really accepted the validity of these criteria, the criteria of economic achievement, social progress, and democratic mores. Many of the old intelligentsia did not, so the differences of French Canada on this score never bothered them. For the new intelligentsia, there was an acute problem. Insofar as they identified themselves as French Canadians, they were nagged by a sense of collective inferiority in those fields that they prized. This was indeed one of the factors lying behind the strange ambivalence in attitude which many of the new intelligentsia showed: under Duplessis they were rabidly antinationalist; under the new regime they were just as rabidly nationalist. In many cases, this was because they had tried both identifications – as North Americans first, in opposition to the ghetto psychology of those who followed the Duplessis regime, and then as something over and against English North America. In both cases, the identification was uneasy and was therefore accompanied by a violence of attitude and a strong rejection of the other identification. In fact, it was impossible for any but a small minority of French Canadians to take the identification as North Americans successfully over the long run, for only a small minority had a good enough command, not only of the English language but of the Anglo-Saxon North American way of life, to feel that they did not suffer in comparison with Texans and Ontarians.

The new nationalism reflected the widespread identification of the new intelligentsia as French Canadians over and against the North American norm. The strains that this produced, the strains of comparison between French Canada and the rest of North America on the criteria mentioned above, led to a strong desire for reform in just those fields, reforms that would make French Canada an economically dynamic society, a progressive society, and a fully democratic society. It is reforms of this kind that were undertaken to some extent by the Lesage regime.

But such was the nature of this nationalist sentiment that it was not enough that these reforms come about. They had to be brought about by the society itself and to be purely its own responsibility; for the type of desire provoked by the comparison was the desire to prove oneself, and this is by definition a goal that cannot be attained with outside help. Hence, the widespread demand was not only for modernizing reform but for modernizing reform carried out by French Canada, and since this type of reform requires an increased intervention by the state, and since the state concerned had to be identified as a French-Canadian state, the logic of the demand led to the strengthening of the state of Quebec – and, in the limiting case, independence for the state of Quebec. Naturally, the pressures described above, those suffered by French Canadians working in English-dominated industry, tended to generate demands of the same kind, demands that the economy of Quebec be francized. But since the greater part of industries were owned by English Canadians or Americans, it was natural that this demand take the form of state intervention to create a French sector to the economy, either by public enterprise or by state support of French private enterprise; this in turn led to a demand for the strengthening of the state and, of course, of a state that could be identified as French – that is, the government at Quebec rather than that at Ottawa.

THE REAL WORLD OF FACTS

Can we find some empirical confirmation for the above analysis? I have maintained that the new nationalism, which found its most far-reaching expression in the idea of an independent Quebec, was mainly a middle-class phenomenon, largely the creation of the intelligentsia, and that its roots were to be found partly in the situation of this class, competing for promotion and careers in a modern economy that was in origin and stamp largely Anglo-Saxon, and partly in this class's perception of the way in which French-Canadian society compared with Anglo-Saxon North America. These three theses are obviously closely linked. If I am right about the origins of modern nationalism here, it follows that the thesis about its social locus is correct, for the two preoccupations mentioned are eminently middle-class ones. Although workers sometimes felt the disadvantages of working for employers who could not speak their language, and although they even had their possibilities of promotion to, say, foreman, affected by this, the difficulties inherent in Anglo-Saxon economic dominance affected fewer of them and in less important ways than their compatriots on the cadre or management level. In addition, the frictions on the shop level could be avoided more easily by relatively simple reforms (for example, by having French-speaking personnel managers) than could the subtle frustrations and strains which employees on higher levels suffered.

Secondly, the preoccupation with the problem of identity, although not confined to the middle classes, was much stronger there than it was lower in the social scale. If I have analysed this feeling correctly, it must have grown as face-to-face contact with the outside group increased. This, too, was generally greater among cadre and management personnel than among workers. Where French-speaking workers had contact with English-speaking people, it was with English workers; but workers of both cultures felt their status to be defined more by their common condition than by their culture. Culture became a factor only when it counted in the competition for jobs (in the same way that it featured, for instance, in the hostility sometimes shown towards immigrants). The middle-class people, on the other hand, identified themselves more readily with the achievement, or lack of it, of their cultural group and felt themselves more easily exalted or diminished by it. In addition, where French-speaking employers were concerned, French workers often had an experience of these people which did not predispose them to wish for an increase of the breed. This was understandable, since French business was often small business and undercapitalized business, and this always spells lower wages and worse conditions than big business.

What, then, is the evidence for this complex of propositions? I referred above to the survey undertaken in 1963 by the Groupe de recherche sociale, testing attitudes to separatism. This survey was taken on a 1000-person sample among French-speaking Quebeckers. I quote the results as published in *Maclean's* magazine of 2 November 1963.

Of the mainly middle-class nature of the separatist sentiment the survey left little doubt. We can see this in the answers to the question concerning the respondents' stand on separatism. The percentage of those in favour for the whole sample was 13. If we define the middle class here as an intelligentsia, as I have suggested, the thesis is borne out. Among those who had completed only primary education, separatism was supported by 11 per cent; the figure for those with only secondary education was the same;

but among those with special or technical training, 29 per cent favoured separation, and for graduates of university or *collège classique* the figure was 26 per cent. If we define social class by income, the same pattern is visible: for incomes below $1999 the figure of favourables was 9 per cent; among those earning $2000 to $2999 it rose to 12 per cent; from $3000 to $4999 it attained 14 per cent; in the bracket $5000 to $5999 it dropped to 13 per cent; and among those earning $6000 and over, 26 per cent were in favour of separatism.

As far as the other theses are concerned, the findings of the survey are less immediately relevant. Indeed, in one case they might be seen to point the other way. My belief that one of the roots of nationalism was the situation of French Canadians in the upper reaches of a Quebec economy dominated by Anglo-Saxon North America is somewhat dented by the breakdown of favourables according to occupation. "Professionals and similar groups" were 25 per cent in favour, but "managers, senior civil servants, small businessmen" were only 10 per cent behind separation. In my defence, however, I can point to the fact that this category is much too heterogeneous. Insofar as it includes provincial bureaucrats, for instance, it touches on a group working in a homogeneous French environment. The same can be said for some small business. More significant, I believe, is the figure for students in favour of separatism: 25 per cent. These were those who were on the point of entering the upper echelons of the economy, who were about to step on the lowest rungs of a ladder whose top, theoretically, was the summit.

The difficulty with all these figures is that they do not bear specifically on this one thesis. The high figure for students, for instance, can also be explained (and, I maintain, should also be explained) by the second factor, the malaise surrounding the problem of identity. Here one can say only that the results are compatible with this view but do not force it on us. Thus, separatism enjoyed more favour in Montreal (16 per cent), where there was a high degree of contact with English Canada, than it did in the rest of the province (11 per cent). The high figure among professional groups is not incompatible, either, with our thesis. Among farmers, who had generally the least contact, only 8 per cent favoured separation.

There is, however, one anomaly in those figures broken down by occupation. While only 12 per cent of skilled workers and craftsmen were in favour, the figure for unskilled workers was 16 per cent. This would seem to indicate that purely economic discontents were also a contributing factor. This I am not inclined to believe. This 16 per cent remains hard to explain in itself, as it were, for there was no corresponding bulge in the figures broken down by income, cited above. There, the popularity of separatism increased according to the rise in the social scale. As for a subsidiary hypothesis in the above text, to the effect that social mobility was a factor making for nationalism, that the two factors weighed more with those recently risen in the social scale, there was unfortunately no available evidence either way.

The main theses of my study, however, seem to have some basis when we look at the ideology that emerged as the dominant one in modern Quebec nationalism. There was, of course, a broad spectrum of opinion among nationalists. There were the old corporatists for whom Salazar's Portugal remained the promised land, and there were vocal and enthusiastic Castrists. But certain dominant strands can yet be seen to emerge. Like much of modern nationalism, the Quebec phenomenon is hard to classify in left-right terms. Being focused on the problems of development in an economy dominated by foreigners, it naturally looked to a large role for the state in the economy. This is what gave it a leftist air and what made it highly tolerant of the left (in its initial stages) – this, together with the "anticolonialist" rhetoric which it spontaneously tried to assimilate to the Quebec context.

Yet as the form of state intervention sought became clearer, differences began to appear which marked the movement off from the classical left, in the democratic West at least, and which bespoke its middle-class origin and the preoccupations that gave rise to it. In the light of what has been said above, we should expect state intervention to be prized by nationalists to the extent that it would fulfil one or both of two goals: to francize the economy, thus opening up more jobs in which French Canadians could operate in their own language; and to give proof of the growing power or increase the prestige of the French-Canadian community, thus easing the malaise connected with the problem of identity.

Both these goals were in evidence in the reform program of the Lesage government, and particularly in the measures most widely hailed in nationalist circles. Thus, the nationalization of electricity, which was the main issue of the 1962 provincial election, was largely calculated, along with its utility as an accretion of planning power, to increase the French-speaking sector of the economy. It was frequently pointed out that the existing public sector of the power industry was run in French and staffed by French personnel, which had not been the case prior to its takeover in 1944. This seemed a convincing ground for nationalizing the rest. Again, the projected steel complex was seen by the educated public largely as a prestige venture; although its employment-creating effects may not have been as great as some government spokesmen claimed, there was clearly a widespread desire to believe in the efficacy of the venture because of its immense prestige as a symbol of industrial maturity.

It is clear that this seeking of more high-level jobs, coupled with prestige, can provide the motive for a great many reforms that are traditionally understood as leftist, especially in a society that has been very backward in certain respects and has a great deal to catch up with simply in terms of efficiency. Thus, the national awakening certainly contributed to the creation of a ministry of education in an attempt to wrest education from the control of the antediluvian clerical machinery which had hitherto governed it in Quebec.

But a nationalist policy distinguishes itself from a traditional policy of the left partly by its aims and partly by the transformations that it is capable of undergoing. In the first respect, it concentrates on a policy of development with an eye more to national greatness than to welfare benefits. What are known as welfare measures therefore have a relatively low priority, although they are not actively opposed. If we compare the Lesage government in Quebec with the CCF government in Saskatchewan, we can see the difference. The CCF set up the first hospitalization scheme on the continent, the first medicare scheme, and so on. The Lesage government applied hospitalization belatedly to Quebec when it came to office, and it later announced its intention to institute a pension scheme. Characteristically, though, this was seen more as a means of acquiring development funds than as a social security measure. This exhausted the immediate concerns of the government in this field. Of course, the goal of development with a low priority on welfare fits another stream in the traditional left, namely bolshevism. But it is enough to raise the comparison to see its inappropriateness. Stalin's development was built on the graves of a previous ruling class. This was far from being the aim in Quebec. Indeed, it was feared that the policy of grand development might fail in its purpose because of a too great coddling of the local bourgeoisie.

In the second respect, I have spoken of the transformations of which the policy was capable. No policy of a living movement is static; it is changing over time and in response to the conditions it meets. An important way to define a policy is in terms of the transformations it could undergo. What would it mean to radicalize a given policy, for instance, if those who supported it saw a worsening of the evils it was meant to cure? In this way policies superficially similar in their moderate forms can be distinguished. With a policy of the left, when the ills it is trying to meet become more acute, it typically moves to increased economic initiative by the state and to a challenge to the social position of the economically dominant classes. This is what "being more left" means. In the Quebec context, a greater sense of the urgency of the problems produced a radicalization of a different kind. The more extreme policy was politically more extreme, demanding the concentration of political power in French hands – that is, in the hands of the dominant classes in French Canada – but socially it was often less extreme, turning away from divisive internal reforms or devoting less attention to them. This was even in a sense true of the extreme left of nationalism, of the Castrist stamp such as the *Parti pris* group. Of course, social radicalism was here covered in nationalist terms by the image of the Anglo-Saxon exploiter. But *Parti pris* also claimed to be against the local bourgeoisie, and this was its claim to the title "leftist." Yet while rigid theoretically in its rejection of bourgeois thought, *Parti pris* often envisaged without scandal tactical alliances with bourgeois nationalism, even accepting a right-wing dictatorship if this was to be a necessary phase on the path to independence.

In terms of its capacity for transformation, therefore, Quebec nationalism revealed itself once again to be a middle-class phenomenon and distinct from the traditional left. In its moderate form, it came close to part of the traditional left-wing program. But when one radicalized it – that is, observed the form it took in the minds of those who saw the root problems as more acute than the moderates did – the element of internal reform diminished, and the concentration was on the reality or the symbolic trappings of political power, namely, independence. Indeed, separatism was often the ideology of those who saw the plight of French Quebec in sombre terms.

CONCLUSION

Can one presume to put forward some general hypotheses about nationalism which could be tested in confrontation with modern history? I would say, first, that modern nationalism is primarily a middle-class phenomenon, particularly of that part of the middle class that is highly educated; that it tends to appear where the middle class of a less developed society becomes integrated into the modern international economy or aspires to do so through emulation; that it often grows with social mobility, both because the integration of a middle class into the international economy often goes with the rise of a new class and because people recently risen feel the strains of the problem of identity more acutely; and that the more the indigenous middle class accepts the values of the advanced economy, the greater is the nationalist emotion.

Modern nationalism will, therefore, present a visage often resembling that of the traditional left. But it will differ from it in program, being less sensitive to the welfare issues that have been the staple diet of at least Western social democracy, and it will differ in what I have called the transformations of which it is capable; in a pinch, it is the political sovereignty of the society wielded by the existing ruling groups that counts more than the reforms. On this view, also, we can hazard the hypothesis that nationalism has little intrinsic appeal to classes lower in the social order, workers or peasants; it appeals only when it is linked with the solution of deeply felt economic ills, often by the presentation of the nationalist goal as a messianic solution to all social and economic ills. This identification succeeds with the masses in certain conditions, which are hard to determine exactly, and then nationalism becomes a mass force. This has not yet happened in Quebec, although there are signs that it might. If it does, Quebec will accede to independence in a short space of time.

CHAPTER TWO

A Canadian Future?

In 1961 the New Democratic Party (NDP) succeeded the Co-operative Commonwealth Federation (CCF) as the political vehicle of the Canadian left. Charles Taylor – a young academic in his early thirties, fresh from Oxford – swiftly became one of the main leaders of the party in Quebec, and he held the position of federal vice-president of the NDP from 1966 to 1971. An unsuccessful candidate in four elections, he was defeated by Pierre Elliott Trudeau in the riding of Mount Royal in 1965. To some extent, Taylor's failure was also the failure of attempts to reconcile the French- and English-Canadian conceptions of federalism and nationhood. The following text is taken from his *Pattern of Politics* (1970). Starting from the philosophical parameters of civic humanism, Taylor paints a picture of the future that Canada could experience if it learned to express and objectify in its institutions and public places both the need for unity that is felt by some of its citizens (English-speaking Canadians, who fear the American leviathan) and the desire for autonomy of others (French Canadians, who are wary of an attempt to level their identity). After lucidly dissecting the secessionist aspirations of the various social classes of Quebec, Taylor expresses the wish that the Canadian political system will prove flexible.

THE ATTEMPT TO CREATE A DIALOGUE SOCIETY – or any other new, important departure – cannot even be begun in Canada without coming to grips with the emotionally explosive problems of our

Taken from *The Pattern of Politics* (Toronto: McClelland & Stewart, 1970).
Used by permission of the Canadian Publishers, McClelland & Stewart.

national existence, of our unity and "identity" as a country. To these I now turn. It is not easy to do justice to these problems – not just because of their complexity or the tension they generate but because of the very duality of the country which lies at the base of so many of them. The "two solitudes" of Hugh MacLennan are still a fundamental reality in Canada; the ways that the two groups envisage their predicament, their problems, and their common country are so different that it is hard to find a common language. They are like two photographs of the same object taken from such different points of view that they cannot be superimposed.

As a consequence, when speaking of the problem of Canadian unity, one often finds oneself talking in a purely English-Canadian perspective, or a purely French-Canadian perspective – depending on one's interlocutor and context. In what follows, let me try to surmount this difficulty by deferring to it at the outset and by speaking first in one perspective and then in the other. Let me try to draw out of both some understanding of the common predicament and common goals.

DARING TO DARE

English Canadians have been and are today very concerned with the problem of Canadian unity. They have also been concerned with what used to be called the question of Canadian "identity," and although the word has passed out of currency, the problem remains. Simply put, it is the question of what it is to be a nation and whether Canada has it. This problem is made more acute by our close contact with our giant neighbour to the south, not because, as some unsympathetic observers (such as Quebec separatists) would have it, English Canadians find it hard to distinguish themselves from Americans – because in very important respects they are not alike – but because Americans set a very definite and obtrusive standard of what it is to be a country. The United States is supposedly founded upon certain definite ideas and is said to exist for them. Americans differ deeply and passionately about how to interpret these ideas, but this simply casts into sharper relief the central position that they occupy and the common belief that the United States represents a new (and, for some, definitive) civilization. (It is no accident that one may read the proud motto, *novus ordo seculorum*, "a new order of time," on the American dollar bill.) The dialogue within the United States is carried out by what purports to be a reference to values of Lockeian liberalism, the traditional foundation of the American Way. Everybody from the hippy to the Bircher argues his case from the premise of the individual's freedom to pursue happiness in his own way. The importance and world significance of these values are doubted by few, even though America's world mission is seen very differently by hawks and doves.

Faced with this model, it is natural for Canadians to wonder whether we have an identity. For we have not and could never have one of this kind. In this respect we are more like a European country; that is, we have a greater ideological spread in our politics, and no one set of ideas can be held up to be "Canadian values" or to be the foundation of a "Canadian way of life." A Committee on Un-Canadian activities could only be a joke at the expense of our neighbours. But if the American model does not fit, the European one does not either; for these nations are for the most part united by language, by culture, and often by a long history. In Canada these things serve rather to divide. Once we were officially known as British North America, and this may have given many British Canadians a sense of what they were; but this label automatically excluded the rest – new Canadians and French Canadians. However, this pro-British sentiment is dying out. As for language and culture being points of diversity, no further comment is needed. But in Canada even history divides. The sharing of great events usually welds a nation together, but these in Canada have as often as not been moments of acute inner conflict: the Riel rebellion and the two world wars (which brought about two conscription crises) were sources of division rather than unity. The only model for a state like Canada that remains seems to be the multilingual European state, such as Belgium or Switzerland. But this is hardly helpful. Belgium is ripped by even worse internal conflict between language groups than Canada is, and Switzerland seems to achieve harmony by the device of mutual ignorance in watertight cantons. (The exception is Berne, which has its own knotty separatist problem in the Juras.) We Canadians are thus very much on our own. We have to create our own model.

In fact, the search for identity seems to be at odds in Canada with the search for national unity; for our country is very diverse – not only in the obvious sense, that there are two major languages and cultures, or in the "mosaic" sense, that there are people from many different backgrounds, but in the geographical and historical sense. Even within "English" Canada, there are great differences between, say, the Maritimes (not to speak of Newfoundland) and what Maritimers often call "Upper Canada," which in turn differs greatly from the Prairies. And for all people east of the Rocky Mountains, British Columbia is a strange place, not quite believable. These differences are not just ones of regional separation and economic interest, but are often based on history, background, and tradition.

Many of Canada's constituent groups or regions have a strong sense of identity. The case hardly has to be made for French Canada, but it can easily be made for the Maritimes, Newfoundland, British Columbia – to mention only indisputable areas of strong feeling. This is not to say that the people of these regions now define themselves more in terms of their local identity than as Canadians – just that if they were thrust on their own, the problem of "identity" would not arise for them (though that of annexation might, but that is a different matter). The problem of identity arises only for the whole enterprise of which all these are parts. And the concern about Canadian identity is partly also a concern for unity, a questioning of what it is that really holds us together.

As we saw, British Canadians had no identity problem. But that was at the expense of the non-British Canadians who had to suffer the King, the Empire, and all the rest. British North America is passing; but its successor, the more polyglot "English" Canada, has inherited its intolerance towards the rights of the French language. Fortunately there are signs that this, too, is changing and that many English Canadians now not only accept but value cultural duality. And one hears it said that what makes Canada unique and worthwhile is just this – that it is not an English country but is what in the jargon of today we call a bicultural country.

The mere belated acceptance of difference is not enough to provide the real basis of unity in this country. It will remove some of the sources of friction, but it will not create a strong sense of common fate and common belonging – in other words, an identity that will also unite Canadians. Divided as we are by language, culture, tradition, provenance, and history, we can only be brought together by common purposes; our unity must be a projective one, based on a significant common future rather than a shared past. And this, of course, is the great truism of Canadian history, that the country has only come alive in periods in which people have had a strong feeling of collective enterprise, such as the first periods of transcontinental settlement. But to approach things from this angle is unsatisfactory, for it sounds as though a common purpose will justify itself simply because it creates unity, as though we were looking for a purpose, any purpose. In fact, a set of goals will only do the job of uniting us to the extent that they can command allegiance and enthusiasm in their own right. Otherwise the whole thing would be a charade.

Today, common purposes of some considerable moment do lie at hand, soliciting us, as it were. The fact that we introduce these into the context of a discussion on Canadian unity and bring to the fore the role they can play cannot really hide from us their intrinsic value. In fact, three important common goals arise from our situation. The first is the building of a bicultural society, not just in the sense of a society in which the rights of both languages are respected, but in the sense of a society (very rare in today's world) in which both groups can learn from each other and be enriched by living side by side. This country is one of the few that can show the world how to make diversity a source of richness, from the diversity between francophone and anglophone to the lesser one between Canadians of different backgrounds and cultures of origin. Canada is a natural locus for the experiment in the dialogue society.

The second common goal is the particular role Canada has to play in the world. Without exaggerating our importance, which for a while in the postwar period seemed greater than it was, we should accept the fact that Canada – as an advanced, very rich country, in good standing in the West and yet also trusted in Africa and Asia (though virtually unknown in Latin America) – can do certain jobs of contacting and mediation which few other powers are as well-equipped to do. Canadians can play a circumscribed but nevertheless very useful role in the United Nations. We should play this role to the hilt, although to do this will take some courage, for it will require that we change our priorities and spend less on defence and more on aid; that we reorient our remaining defence effort towards the United Nations; and, above all, that we at least sink no further into satellite status beside the United States – and this in turn presupposes that we take some measures to reverse our growing economic dependence on the United States.

But there is a third goal, which is even more urgent to Canadian unity, and that is the creation of a more egalitarian society. Canada suffers from great inequalities, not just between different social classes but also between regions, and this certainly puts a strain on our unity, creating a sense of regional alienation. This goal calls for a program of regional development and planning the like of which has not been attempted on this continent. We would have to look to Europe for models, to Norway or Italy. Serious regional development – like that undertaken by the Italian government – would mean the large-scale use of government-controlled investment funds. (Once again, a body such as the Canada Development Corporation can be seen to be an essential instrument of planning.) This is no small task. To bring genuine equality in living conditions right across Canada would be an immense realization – beside which the railway epic of the last century would pale into insignificance.

Canadians do not lack vital, common purposes. But we have a problem nonetheless. These three goals, while they would form an imposing basis for unity in one way, would also divide the country in another, for they constitute a challenge to things as they are. The battleline on the first goal will be largely between those in English Canada who have still not really accepted the French fact, or have still not accepted it outside the "reservation" of the Province of Quebec, and those who see Canada as a country with a dual culture. The line of division is partly regional and ethnic, but also partly one of age. Ontarians, Anglo-Saxons, and the young are more ready to accept the French fact; Westerners, new Canadians, and the old are relatively less sympathetic. To the degree that the difference is one of age and information, one can hope that this division will be overcome in time and will give way to a new unanimity around the institutions of a bicultural society.

The other goals raise a different order of challenge. They call for planning, for recovery of our economic independence from the United States, and hence for a challenge to corporate autonomy. And this cannot fail to give rise to the kind of divisions that we have called polarized politics. The seeming paradox of our situation is that really meaningful unity can only be attained by another kind of division. But this is no real paradox. People of different regions, backgrounds, languages, and cultures can only come together around some common project; and if this is meaningful and not some magic consensus-dream in which we can all project what we want, it is bound to inconvenience somebody and thus raise opposition. The great transcontinental railroads were, in their day, great bones of contention.

In contemporary Canada, the élites of politics, business, education, and certain other professions have contacts across the country. But farmers and blue-collar or white-collar workers in Quebec, say, have only a dim inkling of what their counterparts are like in other provinces, and little sense that they have much of significance in common with them. A program of reform that comes to grips with certain common problems could create a sense of common purpose across these barriers; but it would at the same time divide Canadians within all regions and groups along the lines of their political option. A division between left and right would tend to close the gap between French and English, Easterner and Westerner.

For those who believe in consensus politics, this would be just to jump from the frying pan into the fire. But I have been arguing all along that the politics of polarization, far from being an evil, is the only way in which certain very meaningful issues can come to the fore and certain important reforms can be attempted. It makes for a much more meaningful political dialogue between genuinely different views, rather than the elaborate *pas de deux* where one party says B because the other says A, when it could just as easily have been the other way round. But in Canada, polarized politics is more than a good; it is an essential condition of a more meaningful unity, and perhaps even of survival.

Yet it is resisted for various reasons: the hold of consensus politics, the strength of the corporate mystique, and the fear of American retaliation. What must also be admitted is a certain sense we have of American superiority in these matters. The unspoken belief of many is that if something has not been tried in the United States, it probably is not worth trying. This is reflected in, among other things, the large number of borrowings from across the border and in the number of good ideas that cannot get a hearing here until they are tried out there – for example, the Company of Young Canadians and the War on Poverty (declared but never fought). Even the cult of the New Young Leader leans on its American precedents, and the left replies to this with the New Left politics of alienation, which is a straight import.

This complex of imitation is itself a syndrome that arises from our uncertain and weak sense of common purpose, and so it sets up a kind of vicious circle whereby the will to undertake an enterprise of significance is sapped by this fear of innovating beyond the canonical limits provided by the American model, while in turn this fear is fed by the sparseness of our achievements. Once in a while we pull off something like Expo '67, where someone dared to throw out New York as a model, and the result is a sudden heightened sense of capacity. But we will need more than a few such shots in the arm before this terrible pusillanimity can be overcome.

English Canada remains poised between the tempting prospects of original creative change and the old fears of innovation. This is one reason for the great success of Trudeaumania. It provided the ideal psychological compromise between these two contradictory drives. The Trudeau image offered all the excitement of change, the "spirit of Expo" and all that, while offering the reassurance – which the average man could read in the benign reactions of power and privilege – that no serious challenge would be offered to the way things are. The act looked terrific, but everyone knew that no crockery was going to be broken. Everyone could relax and indulge the yearning for change without arousing the fear of novelty. This is, of course, the principle of all wish-fulfilment. The secret of Trudeaumania was to use this very effectively as a political instrument.

BETWEEN NATION AND STATE

The hang-ups of English Canadians – a people who are not quite sure if they dare to dare – seem at first sight strangely and disturbingly paralleled in French Canada. French Canada has, of course, no problem of identity. The sense of what French Canadians are as a group is strong enough to be relatively untouched, even by big changes in the accepted definitions. For instance, the confessional element, which played a big role in the self-image of many French Canadians in previous generations, though never of all of them, is now declining in the community's definition of itself. This has not happened without struggle, but at no time has there been anything like a crisis of identity even for those who have entirely broken with the church. The sense of being a French Canadian is more fundamental than any of its definitions. Again, the older, more tribal attitude, which defined a French Canadian by ancestry ("O Canada, terre de nos aïeux"), is now giving way to an open definition that includes all "francophones" – again, without causing a ripple in the basic sense of identity. (Perhaps this is because there are still so few foreign-born francophones in Quebec.)

The vast majority of French Canadians have a basic identification with what has been appropriately called *la nation canadienne-française.* This is far more important and fundamental to them than their being part of the political entity called Canada. It is a reflection of the continuing gap between the two solitudes that this fact still is not generally accepted in English Canada in the double sense of the term – that is, English Canadians generally do not know it, nor can they reconcile themselves to the fact when it is demonstrated to them. The visit of Charles de Gaulle in 1967 provided a distressing illustration of this.

In fact, both sides have a way of playing unconsciously on the fears of the other, resembling nothing so much as a marriage of neurotics. For English Canadians, who are acutely aware of the diversity of the country, of the tenuous and indefinable nature of what holds it together, the question of unity is paramount. For any part of Canadian society to demonstrate that it prizes its part over the whole smacks of treason. If this feeling is generalized, the English Canadian argues, the place will break up. So any demonstration that *la nation canadienne-française* is the fundamental gut-loyalty of French Canadians fills English Canadians with anxiety. They call stridently for unity. French Canadians, for their part, have a long experience of being dragged into things, including wars and the like, by a larger and more powerful partner; and when English Canada gets in a let's-all-get-together-and-tighten-unity mood, French Canadians get nervous. An aroused English Canada bent on whipping everyone into line is associated with too many painful memories. The reflexes of autonomism come to the fore. This, in turn, further incenses the English Canadians, and so we go around again.

If French Canadians must learn to understand the English anxiety about unity, English Canadians must learn that the identification with *la nation canadienne-française* is not at all the antechamber to separatism. It does not mean that French Quebeckers, for instance, basically identify with the State of Quebec as their political instrument. All this is the superstructure built by the political élites. The extreme positions capture the lion's share of press, radio, and television coverage – but since when have extremes reflected basic popular attitudes? The point about these popular attitudes is that they are not political; they cannot be adequately expressed in any political or constitutional formula. These formulae are constantly being concocted with an endless fertility by the élites. But none really reflects mass feeling. This goes as much for federalist as for separatist theories. The popular attitude is encapsulated in the use of the term *Canadiens*, which was traditionally used for French Canadians. The new separatist attempt to make people identify as Québécois is as distinct from this as the identification with the whole country, regardless of language, which is part of the meaning of the English word "Canadian."

This resistance of the mass of Quebeckers to separatist blandishments has, however, complex motives. In one way – and this is where the analogy with English-Canadian hang-ups comes in – it is based on a fear of the consequences. The economic dangers of separatism do not need to be spelled out for most Quebeckers. Indeed, they are, if anything, overestimated by the population; and this because of the deep-lying belief that the *anglais* (or American) is the irreplaceable bringer of jobs and hence of prosperity.

To many French Canadians, separatism means simply that the anglophone goes, and with him the jobs he gives. The sense of dependence is one of the prime targets of separatist intellectuals, who berate this attitude as a vestige of "colonialism." In this sense, separatism means an affirmation of collective confidence.

But such is the ambiguity of motive here that the reverse is also true; for part of the resistance to separatism springs from an obscure sense that one's habitat is the whole country. And here the separatists attack the illusion that French Canadians can ever be at home in a land dominated by English, and they call on everyone to focus their loyalty on the only society they can control. The shoe is now on the other foot; here it is separatism that is based on fear and the psychology of perpetual defeat. That this is a powerful motive in separatism can be seen from the continued reference to adverse demographic developments. A good part of the drive for unilingualism in Quebec is powered by the fear of assimilation, even in Montreal. A large-scale exodus of anglophones is actively desired.

Both separatism and the resistance to it are an ambiguous mixture of affirmation and fear. But from the fact that the popular sentiment resists separatism, we cannot conclude that the people are committed to federalism in any kind of structured way. It is a feeling rather than an idea, but insofar as it can be defined, it is a kind of instinct that French Canada exists and must exist on two levels: as a French nation in Canada as a whole, but also as expressed in the only French province, Quebec. The existence of Quebec as a heartland is essential to the existence of the whole. And, indeed, this is nothing more than the unvarnished truth, for a great many of the institutions which also serve the minorities, such as Radio-Canada, would not exist if there were not a majority French society somewhere in this country. Thus, while French Canada is more than Quebec, the province will always be instinctively accorded a "special status" in French Canada.

In relation to this feeling, the various ideological formulae between which Quebeckers have been asked to choose represent radical oversimplifications. Both René Lévesque and Pierre Trudeau offered a radical solution that would do away with one of the dimensions in which French Canadians have operated for a century. Lévesque wanted to do away with the Canadian dimension;

Trudeau's image was of French-speaking Canadians as individuals without the collective dimensions of identification with *la nation canadienne-française*. Both positions have had great appeal because they are easy to present. But most people are still relatively unimpressed by logic. They simply sense they are being asked to give up something without valid reason.

The ordinary people of Quebec thus fight a kind of political guerrilla war with the educated élite of the province. The latter have in recent years been obsessed with constitutional issues, offering an unending stream of formulae: separatism, associate statehood, different versions of special status, One Canada without special status, and so on. In spite of tireless explanation and propaganda, the mass of the population have stubbornly refused to choose one at the expense of all the rest. They have usually voted autonomist on the provincial level, but this is without prejudice to their vote on the federal level (which, alas, often goes like that of most minorities to the side with the biggest battalions). In this way the proponents of almost all constitutional options can claim victory at some time or other, and the people rest happy in the assurance that all the options remain open.

But this familiar scenario cannot be counted on to repeat itself indefinitely. There are some factors that could shake things loose and make separatism more of a live option. One would be a mass conversion away from the idea that the English are essential to prosperity, and to the opposite idea that they are the source of all woes. In spite of the general popularity of scapegoat arguments, this development is not likely, if only because the sense of the indispensability of *les anglais* is very strong. More serious is the fact that the balance between the élite, as defined in terms of education, and the rest of the population has been changing. As French Canada modernizes, it will – like similar societies – enjoy a higher and higher proportion of trained and educated people. The difference is even more striking if one looks at the population by age group. For example, the rising generation in 1970 contained a proportion of the highly educated which vastly exceeded all previous ones. And separatism – or, in general, preoccupation with this type of issue – was at its strongest among the young and educated. What will be the mood of a society in which the young and educated count for much more? Which way will they ultimately turn?

The answer depends to a great extent on what we do with the common purposes discussed earlier. The resistance to separatism, as I said above, is made up of both positive and negative elements, of both affirmation and fear. This will probably always be the case, but a lot will depend on the balance between the two elements in people's minds. The young people who passed through university in 1970 were in some degree reacting against the attitudes of their elders, for whom federalism was almost entirely a prudential affair. This inglorious stance and the weak accommodating attitudes that went with it inspired the contempt of the younger generation. The continuance of Canada may therefore depend on our giving a more meaningful content to the positive sense of being part of a bigger country, which most Quebeckers still feel.

THE PROJECT OF UNITY

This is where action on the common purposes mentioned above, and particularly on the third, could be crucial for the future of Canada. Suppose, for instance, that we begin to tackle the problem of regional development as we never have before and that we use to this end the kind of resources that could be mobilized by the country as a whole through the federal Canada Development Fund. Investment resources, which are now pre-empted by large private corporations or invested in safe bonds by insurance companies, could be channelled into the neglected areas of eastern Quebec and the Maritimes to back up provincial development plans and give the financial backing that is essential to foster their centres of growth. We could then repeat on the Atlantic seaboard of Canada something of the "miracle" that the Italian government brought about in southern Italy.

Suppose that we channelled resources from defence and from lower-priority private investment into provincial education budgets, and into housing and urban redevelopment in our major metropolitan centres. In this context, belonging to Canada would be significant as it never has been before. The struggle to achieve these goals – and there would unquestionably be a struggle, both within Canada and in resistance to American corporate power – would open a new frontier for the great energy and idealism of that mass of young Quebeckers who are deeply dissatisfied with the status quo. At the moment, the only exciting and challenging idea is that of independence; it is neutralized largely by the instinctive prudence of the majority. But things could be very different if Canada were something more than an insurance policy, if it were the locus of action that tackled the problems that really touch people's lives. We could conduct negotiations within the framework of a common political will and with some idea of what we want to do together.

What may have looked like a disturbing parallel between English and French Canada, both of which want independence but fear to pay the price, now appears in a different light. If we ask, as many separatists do, why the reasons for Quebec's remaining in Canada are not also reasons for Canada's accepting integration with the United States, the answer is twofold. First, a Canada sliding to satellite status would have no say over its fate, no voice in the larger block of which it would be a dependent part; second, it would lose the ability to remain distinctly itself. Neither of these need be true of Quebec's relations to Canada. But to make this answer stick, we have to ensure that these "dis-analogies" really hold – that Quebeckers will have a say in determining the fate of the larger unit to which they belong, and that they can remain themselves. The first condition certainly would not be met if Canada continues its slide to satellite status. All that Quebeckers could be assured of under those conditions would be that English Canadians had no more say than themselves. And this is no answer to those for whom separatism is a way of recovering collective control over some of the important determining conditions of their lives. The second condition of unity – that Quebeckers remain themselves – means the institution of a fully bicultural society in which French-speaking minorities outside Quebec have the same rights as Anglo-Quebeckers and in which federal government agencies are really open to people who operate in both languages. But it also means a flexibility in federal-provincial relations (which is at present not very much in evidence), and this raises the vexed question of a special status for Quebec.

The term "special status" seems to unleash all the anxieties that English Canada feels are bound up in a threat to unity; but what is forgotten in the rush to affirm Canadian unity is that, in showing this kind of rigidity, English Canadians are indeed giving Quebec a special status. In a diverse federation such as ours, with such very different conditions prevailing in the regions, we have always accepted that the role of the federal government may be different in relation to different regions. We have an Atlantic Development Board because of the special development problems of that area; the federal government has a Canadian Wheat Board to market the product of one region, the Prairies; Newfoundland receives special subsidies; and so on.

When it comes to Quebec, attitudes are much more rigid. Quebec's way of being different is different from that of other regions, but those regions also differ from each other. Quebec's case is just as reasonable. What underdevelopment is to the Atlantic provinces, what being a one-crop economy used to mean to the Prairies, being the only French-majority society in this hemisphere is to Quebec. It is therefore inevitable that the province will want to keep a closer control on some areas of government action than other provinces will. When there is a general request for federal aid in financing higher education or for a greater federal role in the building of low-cost housing and urban development (to take two examples, one past and one future), it is inevitable and understandable that Quebec will be more nervous of federal intrusion than other provinces will be and that the path of wisdom will be to work out some particular arrangements to meet this special problem. This is, of course, exactly what was done in the case of the Canada and Quebec pension plans. What seemed like an impasse that would have effectively prevented any Canadians from getting a public contributory pension scheme was cleared by a certain flexibility and imagination.

If this flexibility is not forthcoming in the future, it can only serve to paralyse certain programs. In the central area of provincial jurisdiction, which is considered essential for the distinct identity of Quebec – education, some social security, welfare policy, town planning, some aspects of manpower – no Quebec government can be forced to back down. The only way to make the relations of all provinces to the federal government uniform would be to keep the federal government entirely out of anything touching these fields in all provinces. It is not at all clear that this would go down well in English Canada.

It is a paradox that what is presented as a policy for a strong federal government will end up binding its hands in many ways. It will be strong but inactive. In general, we can say that in a diverse federation like ours, the more the central government is active, the more flexible it has to be in its dealings with the different regions. We brought British Columbia into Confederation by promising its people a railroad – the most expensive particular status we ever accorded anyone. The institutions and legislation mentioned above – the Atlantic Development Board, the Canadian Wheat Board, the pension plans – are all fruits of this kind of flexibility.

It is therefore ominous that the mood of English Canada seems set against this. In fact, meaningful unity, as we have seen, can only come through a common purpose, which means much more active government; and this, of course, means greater not less flexibility. But the English-Canadian anxiety over threatened unity will take us in a very different direction; it will frustrate its own goal. This anxiety, like the corresponding separatist obsession with relative population growth and the threat of assimilation, is one of the great negative emotions bedevilling Canadian politics. Where unity requires change and forward movement, this old anxiety pushes English Canadians to conserve the familiar unity of the past. For some, of course, this means the good old days when there was not all this talk about the rights of the French language; but even where it does not bring out the atavistic sense of anglophone superiority, it fosters a rigid antipathy to change. This can all too easily link up with the other resistance to change in English Canada that we noted above, the timidity in face of the corporate mystique and of American hegemony. It is perversely providential that inflexibility towards Quebec necessarily goes with federal inaction. By a delicious coincidence, one can say "no" to Quebec and "no" to change in the same breath.

It is in this context that the idea could really become entrenched among the most sympathetic English Canadians that the problem between our two peoples can be solved by full equality of language rights and that once this hurdle is behind us we can leave the rest more or less as it is. This would be another of those tragic misunderstandings that our two solitudes seem able to generate in inexhaustible supply. For it is not just that various proponents of Quebec autonomy would remain unsatisfied if we stopped there; the real misfortune would be that we would fail to see that we need deeper changes in our politics if we are to draw Quebeckers – and indeed others – more strongly towards the common enterprise that Canada is. For the entire outcome of these negotiations between Quebec, the other provinces, and Ottawa will depend on whether they are carried on in a surrounding atmosphere of alienation between the two groups or in the context of a strong sense of significant common purpose.

CHAPTER THREE

Why Do Nations
Have to Become States?

From 1976 to 1979, Charles Taylor held one of the most prestigious positions in the Anglo-American academic world: he occupied the Chichele chair of social and political theory at Oxford University. His departure for England coincided with the Parti Québécois' accession to power. The following text is the fruit of a paper delivered to the participants of the Canadian Philosophical Association's conference held in Montreal in the spring of 1979, one year before the referendum on sovereignty association. According to Taylor, if national communities want to endow themselves with their very own state, it is chiefly because they want to manage their own affairs. (In 1992 we would say that they "invoke their inherent right of self-government.") The French and American revolutions were carried out by people who wanted to bestow such a homeland upon themselves. However, to understand autonomist and nationalist aspirations among Quebeckers, one must turn to a vocabulary other than that of republican patriotism – namely, that of post-romantic thought. A political community may wish to establish a correspondence between nation and state in order to guarantee room for expression of the language that is a fundamental component of its identity. Its aim in doing so is to create the conditions that will enable it to achieve conclusive results in every sphere of modern life, thus obtaining

Taken from "Why Do Nations Have to Become States?" In *Philosophers Look at Canadian Confederation*, ed. Stanley G. French (Montreal: L'Association canadienne de philosophie, 1979).

the highest forms of recognition. In this text, the reader will find some philosophical foundations of the defence of collective language rights.

THERE ARE THREE MAJOR MODES OF POLITICAL JUSTIFICATION in the modern world: welfare, rights, and self-government. Nationalist modes of thought have become involved in all three and point towards the need for nations to become sovereign states.

THE RISE OF NATIONALISM

The initial locus of nationalism as a political justification was in the context of the aim of self-government. The notion that self-government is a good in itself, that men live a higher life who are part of a free or self-managing people, returns early in the modern world. I say "returns" because it was seen as an ideal that the ancients had lived by and that needed to be recovered. It returns first in Renaissance Italy; Machiavelli stands at the end of the first return of the tradition of civic humanism. We find it again in seventeenth-century England, and it becomes part of the mainstream of European thought in the eighteenth century, with the American and French revolutions. Both look back to republican Rome as their model for a free people. Freedom cannot simply be defined as independence for the individual relative to state interference; it is no longer enough to demand "laissez-faire, laissez-passer." Free people are self-governing people.

This had a natural link with the nascent nationalism. The ancient tradition of civic humanism stressed that self-government was only possible for a community where the members identified strongly with their public institutions, to use modern language, or where men loved the laws, to use the old terminology. Self-government was possible because men were willing to die for the *patria*, for the laws, because they devoted themselves to *res publica*. They had what Montesquieu called virtue. Men who were devoted above all to private goals, or spiritual goals that by-passed the fatherland, were fit politically to live in despotisms but not in a free state. Machiavelli and Rousseau both made this point.

Thus, in both the American and French revolutions, the term for those who were partisans of self-rule was "patriot." This expressed one link between self-government and love of the *patria*.

The idea of a democratic regime where the people lacked such dedication was still foreign to eighteenth-century believers in self-government. But the term expresses the link with modern nationalism, for today it has above all a nationalist ring; we think ironically of patriotism as the motive that may have pushed many Germans to follow Hitler, many Russians to condone Stalin, where the beneficiary of this sentiment is now as much despotism and tyranny as free states. So has the term evolved. Many people even think now of free governments and nationalist feeling as being enemies of one another – in the last analysis, incompatible.

The connection is clear historically. Nationalism did not arise out of the value of self-government. The causes of modern nationalism are very deep and have to do with the erosion of earlier communities and identifications: the withering away of local community, the decline of religious identifications which often bypassed nationality. Indeed, the very notion of a group identification founded on a relation to the supernatural is strange to many moderns in Atlantic civilization; and the local neighbourhood society cannot have the place it once had. But people need a group identification, and the obvious one to take the place of the earlier forms is the one that springs to the attention of the speaking animal, namely, nationality based on language.

But once nationalism arises, it cannot but take the place of patriotism in the aspiration to self-government. Civic humanism needs a strong identification with a community. But this is the form that community-identification takes among modern, emancipated people (emancipated from church, from locality, from hierarchical allegiances). So patriotism comes to mean nationalism. And the context in which nationalism comes first to count politically is that of the call for self-rule. What is demanded here is self-determination. People can only rule themselves if they are grouped in their *patriae*. Only those who form together a *patria* can achieve self-rule, not just any agglomeration of humans who happen to be contiguous with one another. So the ideal demands that *patriae* be given some sort of political personality.

I use the vague term "political personality," rather than saying bluntly that *patriae* ought to be sovereign states, because the eighteenth century already saw our modern dilemma. Its thinkers saw that the close identification with fatherland and the demands of universal participation require a small face-to-face society; whereas modern nations are very large and are spread over vast areas. The solution, as propounded by Montesquieu and Rousseau and as adopted by the nascent United States, was federation – smaller societies joined in a larger union. Both of the political ideas that dispute for the soul of contemporary Quebec were born in the eighteenth century, and from exactly the same source, the aspiration to self-government. This demands that the *patria* be given a political expression. This could be taken to mean independent statehood, sovereignty. But given the size and nature of modern nations, it could also require federation. Of course, these two solutions were not necessarily seen as alternatives. The nation could demand independence and then adopt a federal structure.

The paradigm case is, of course, the United States. The fathers of U.S. independence convinced themselves that they formed a nation, that they could justifiably secede from the English nation to which they had seen themselves until quite recently as belonging (notably when they had fought together against New France, for example, at Louisbourg). They felt justified in this, because they saw themselves as betrayed by their ex-compatriots, denied the rights of Englishmen, relegated to a dependent status. So the modern idea was born. Self-determination is the right of a nation, because it is the condition of self-rule of the people who form the nation. This, either because, since they form a nation, the only *patria* they can identify with is that nation, and hence this must have political expression; or, as in the case of the United States because, since they form a dependent group which can only achieve self-rule by breaking away, freedom demands that they found a *patria* and hence become a nation.

So the first and most important reason why nations had to become states is that it was seen as a condition of self-rule. The demand for the self-determination of nations was thus part of the aspiration to self-government, to popular rule. It was a demand of the left in the nineteenth century. It spread out with the ideas that flowed from the French Revolution. The term "self-determination" was coined later; in the aftermath of World War I it came into its own. And in this age, the desire for it made sense because it was seen as the inevitable condition and concomitant of self-rule. The new nations were achieving self-determination by carving up what had been autocratic or at least authoritarian-ruled empires: Russia, Germany, Austria.

The second great wave of self-determination came after World War II and involved conferring statehood on the ex-colonies of European imperial states. Here, too, self-rule and self-determination were but two sides of the same coin. Or so it was thought. The regimes that now exist in many of the ex-colonies are indeed very far from the tradition of civic humanism and would shock our eighteenth-century forebears (as would many aspects of our own regimes, to say the truth). But even so, the link is not entirely broken. All modern regimes pay obeissance to the ideal of popular rule. All are supposed to be expressions of the popular will, however bogus. All require some formal expression of this through plebiscites or mass elections or other modes of ratification, for the ideal of self-determination is still conceptually inseparable from that of self-rule.

So nations have become states in order to rule themselves. But do they have to? Certainly they do if they are otherwise hopelessly dependent. If you are a colony, you have as a nation no choice. This paradigm predicament is clarified once and for all by the eighteenth-century Americans, and it is repeated endlessly in the period after 1945. This is why the rhetoric of independence slips naturally into the claim that one lives in a colonial predicament. We see this in the language of Quebec nationalists. It can be seen clearly in the terrorism of the Front de libération du Québec (FLQ) – echoing the Algerian Front de libération national (FLN) – but it is also evident among the more sophisticated.[1] Of course, there is some historical truth here. Quebec was a colony. But are we Quebeckers "colonized" now? This would be the shortest way to demonstrate that we must become a sovereign state. Well, we obviously are not in some straightforward sense, not as the Thirteen Colonies were in 1776; nor as, say, India was in 1947.

But it is claimed that there are other forms of dependence, other relations which make it such that the only road to genuine self-rule lies through independence. In order to understand these, we have to look at the other ways in which modern nationalism has become intricated in our political arguments and justifications. Nationalism, I said earlier, is a modern form of group identification, one prevalent among emancipated peoples. But to probe deeper, we would have to say that this very idea of identification, of having an identity, is modern. We can speak anachronistically of the identity of medieval man. But this is anachronistic, because a medieval man did not have the question to which identity is the answer.

The question is "Who am I?" The answer points to certain values, certain allegiances, a certain community perhaps, outside of which I could not function as a fully human subject. Of course, I might be able to go on living as an organism outside any values, allegiance, or even community. But what is peculiar to a human subject is the ability to ask and answer questions about what really matters, what is of the highest value, what is truly significant, what is most moving, most beautiful, and so on. The conception of identity is the view that outside the horizon provided by some master value or some allegiance or some community membership, I would be crucially crippled, would become unable to ask and answer these questions effectively, and would thus be unable to function as a full human subject.

The judgment about identity is a judgment about me in particular, or about some particular person or group. There is no claim that others will be unable to function outside my horizon. The horizon necessary for me is not essential for human beings as such. There are some things which we might judge universally necessary; for instance, a minimum of freedom from crying need or a minimum of love as children. We might argue that without these, no one could become a fully human subject. But the claim about identity is particularized. I may come to realize that belonging to a given culture is part of my identity, because outside of the reference points of this culture I could not begin to put to myself, let alone answer, those questions of ultimate significance that are peculiarly in the repertory of the human subject. Outside this culture, I would not know who I was as a human subject. So this culture helps to identify me.

We can see how the question about identity is a modern one; it belongs to modern, emancipated subjects. For our medieval forebears, there could not have been a question about the conditions of human subjecthood for the individual. In a sense, there were conditions for man as such, especially in his relationship to God, which he could turn his back on with eventually catastrophic results. These conditions were unrecognized or seen only distortedly by pagans and infidels. That was their great misfortune. There was no question of the conditions being different for them. The idea that this can be so is inseparable from modern emancipated humanism. Being human is not just a matter of occupying the rank assigned to humans in the cosmic order. Our humanity is something we each discover in ourselves. To be human is not to be discovered in the order of things in which people are set, but rather in the nature that people discover in themselves. Of course, emancipated humanism does not of itself lead to the notion of identity. It is a necessary but not sufficient condition. The first versions of emancipated humanism of the seventeenth century give us a picture of man as an atomic subject, fulfilling his purposes as a producer and setting up a political order as his instrument. There is as yet no place for the notion of identity, for the question of what horizon of meaning will be essential for this or that person's being human. The need for a horizon of meaning is ignored altogether. Hence, individual and national differences are of no moral relevance.

The sense of the importance of these differences comes in the Romantic period, and it comes with what I have called the question of identity. For each individual to discover in himself what his humanity consists in, he needs a horizon of meaning, which can only be provided by some allegiance, group membership, cultural tradition. He needs, in the broadest sense, a language in which to ask and answer the questions of ultimate significance. The Romantic subject can never be the atomic subject of seventeenth-century thought – of Hobbes and Locke, for instance. Even the most individualistic of Romantic aspirations, in seeing the need for a horizon of meaning, sees that humans are essentially social; for this horizon, this language comes to us within a society. Romantic individualism involves the demand that we break away from group conformity, that we elaborate an original statement; but it has no place for the seventeenth-century myth of the state of nature, the view that we could see our original condition as one of solitary agents of choice.

Since the Romantic insight is that we need a language in the broadest sense in order to discover our humanity, and that this language is something we have access to through our community, it is natural that the community defined by natural language should become one of the most important poles of identification for the civilization that is heir of the Romantics. Romanticism is a deepening of the modern aspiration to what I have called emancipation, to finding one's human purposes in oneself, autonomously, and not in some cosmic and hierarchic order in which we fit. Hence nationalism, the singling out of linguistic nationality as the paradigm pole of self-identity, is part of this modern drive to emancipation. It connects naturally with the demand for self-rule.

At the same time, the Romantic conception of identity, and also therefore nationalism, comes to modify the other modes of political justification that belong to the modern aspiration to emancipation – in terms of welfare and rights. The modern notion of rights is of what has been called "subjective rights." We can speak of subjective rights when we couch our claims about how it is licit and illicit to act in terms of privileges that are seen to belong to subjects. This big change also comes (naturally) in the seventeenth century. Instead of saying, "It is the law of nature that no one ought to take innocent life," we now start to say, "We all have a right to life." This way of putting it makes the norms governing people's behaviour towards us appear as a privilege, as it were, that we own. The point of this semantic transposition of natural law is, first, that it accords us a certain autonomy in deciding how the norms should be applied to us (if I have a right to life, then presumably I can waive it, a possibility which was not allowed by traditional natural law and which the modern theorists felt they had to block by inventing the notion of an "inalienable right"); and, second, that it underscores the dignity of the person. The point of natural law is now seen to be respect for the integrity of human subjects, who are seen as having a certain dignity. Rights talk is plainly part of modern emancipated humanism.

The same is true of modern justifications of welfare. These arise with the principle that the political and other structures in which people are set have no inherent value. People are no longer to be seen as commanding allegiance because they represent the hierarchical order of things, for example, or the chain of being. They are only instruments set up by people to accomplish their purposes. People and their purposes become the only source of

has favoured the economic development of Ontario over Quebec and that the requirements of economic realization must therefore include an independent Quebec government with the major responsibility for the economic management of the province's economy. The argument ramifies greatly. Its relevance is not only to what we have called realization. It is also an argument about welfare: provincial underdevelopment has meant the impoverishment of Québécois, it is claimed. But realization is also an important element in it. I am not concerned here to weigh the argument; I am simply recording it as the form that this mode of justification of sovereignty takes in the present Quebec debate.

Of course, political independence has a more direct relation to realization. Political sovereignty is itself a realization, one that puts a people on the map. This brings us to the third important notion mentioned above. I spoke above about a political status "insulating" Quebec from the invasive influence of North America. Independentists usually object to this kind of language; they protest that their intention is not to turn inward but to have access to the outside world, which they have been denied by being buried as a minority in federal Canada. They touch here on a very important point, which a study of the Romantic conception of identity can also clarify. Because the language/culture that we need for our identity is one that we always receive from others, from our surroundings, it becomes very important that we be recognized for what we are. If this is denied or set at naught by those who surround us, it is extremely difficult to maintain a horizon of meaning by which to identifies ourselves.

This obviously applies to individuals growing up in a community and living their lives in it, but it also applies between communities. This is especially evident when we appreciate how important the self-respect of a culture is. It is gained through realization, but the value of realization depends to a great degree on the recognition of others, on how the people are seen internationally by the world at large. There is therefore among a small people, whose self-confidence has been shaken by living in the shadow of the contemporary world's most powerful language and culture and technology, a tremendous hunger for international recognition. This goes a long way to explain the impact of the famous "Québec libre" speech of General de Gaulle in 1967, which was appreciated far beyond the ranks of independentists.

It can also provide us with another reason for demanding independence, because the formal trappings of sovereignty – the exchange of ambassadors, a seat in the United Nations, and so on – are the paramount form of international recognition today. That is what it means to be internationally recognized. This, incidentally, is why it is very hard to conceive of the independentist movement in Quebec willingly making a deal for a renewed federation short of sovereignty; for the legal status of sovereign country is essential to the goal they seek. This can be caricatured by their enemies as the desire on the part of an élite to ride around in limousines in foreign capitals and cut a figure at international conferences. But it also has a more serious side in the need for recognition, for an acceptance by the world community that one counts for something, has something to say to the world, and is among those addressed by others – the need to exist as a people on the world stage.

WHY NATIONS HAVE TO BECOME STATES

We are now in a position to sum up this rather rambling set of answers to the question "Why should nations become states?" (a) The first answer might be "Because sovereignty is the condition of republican self-rule." This is the answer we can retrospectively put in the mouth of the American independence leaders, except that they had to become a nation at the same time. They made a nation-state, but all in order to rule themselves. It is the answer of the peoples of Central Europe between the wars and of the colonies struggling for liberation after World War II. But it is hard to apply this to our situation. So we turn to (b), another set of arguments that applies to rights. We can argue (i) that the conditions of our identity are indispensable to our being full human subjects; (ii) that, for people today, a crucial pole of identification (in some cases, *the* crucial pole) is their language/culture and hence their linguistic community; thus (iii) the availability of our linguistic community as a viable pole of identification is indispensable to our being full human subjects. Now (iv) we have a right to demand that others respect whatever is indispensable to our being full human subjects (for example, life and liberty). Therefore (v) we have a right to demand that others respect the conditions of our linguistic community being a viable pole of identification.

The conditions mentioned in (v) can be spelled out to include the health and expressive power of our language, a certain realization in crucial sectors on the part of our linguistic community, and some degree of international recognition. These, with other premises, can be made the basis of language legislation such as we now have in Quebec (collective rights), and also of political independence as a matter of right because it is supposedly indispensable to realization and recognition.

What we think of this argument will depend partly on our detailed conception of the conditions mentioned in (v), which may be different from those adumbrated above. But it may also depend on what we think of premises (i), (ii), and (iv). Of these, (ii) is the only controversial one today. It simply states what follows from our definition of identity. One would only challenge this if one wanted to challenge all talk about identity. No doubt many philosophers would, but in fact it is hard to see how much of our modern self-understanding could get on without some concept of this kind. Point (iv) is similarly basic to political thought and argument in the twentieth century.

The big disagreements concern point (ii), whether to affirm or deny it, and if the former, what variant to affirm. Some espouse (ii) in a strong, exclusive form that makes the linguistic community the all-important overriding pole of identity while others see it is an extremely important basis of a modern identity but not the only one. For those such as classical Marxists, the ultimate identity is indeed that of a group, but not a national society; rather, it is the world community of liberated mankind. Proletarians have no country, as the *Communist Manifesto* assures us. Now, for antinationalists of either individual or collectivist stripe, the above argument does not carry through. There is no justification for restrictive language legislation and no justification for sovereignty apart from (a) – its being indispensable for republican self-rule. Since this clearly does not apply to the Quebec-Canada case, the demand is rejected out of hand.

We can see the shape of the battle that is joined between those who affirm (ii) in its most uncompromising form and those who deny it in any form – a battle whose general lines are perhaps distressingly familiar to us. But what if you think, as I do, that neither of these is right? You may not accept that the most important pole of identification is the national one, that making it the only one is liable to stultify human development and justify repressive policies. At the same time, you may not accept that group identification is of no importance at all for our identity; on the contrary, you may think that it is very important for everyone and that in certain circumstances (when the culture is menaced) it can be truly vital. If you also think, as I do, that something like these circumstances have existed in Quebec during the last two centuries, you will have trouble aligning either with the ultranationalists or with the antinationalists. But you can be sure of one thing if you feel like this: the Canadian scene will be perennially frustrating for you, because the extreme positions always seem to win out here. That ultranationalism should win in Quebec is perhaps not too surprising. More surprising is the resistance to it.

What perhaps needs more comment is the antinationalist stand of the rest of Canada. I do not mean by this that there is not a lot of Canadian nationalism around, both healthy and unhealthy. I certainly do not mean to deny that there is a lot of linguistic and cultural narrowness and bigotry in English Canada. From the standpoint of Quebec, we are painfully aware of this. There has certainly been intolerance of the minority – and it is really this, more than anything else, that makes the cause of Canadian unity seem desperate in the long run. But English Canada has not been nationalist in the sense characterized here. The intolerance and bigotry, the suppression of French schools and the French language, were never carried out from a sense of a threatened identity. Indeed, since English Canadians share a language with our giant neighbour, they have rarely had any sense of how language can play a crucial role in identity.

Hence, when faced with the demands of French Canada for some recognition of its rights as a nation, where this took the form of the right of French speakers or the powers and jurisdictions of

Quebec, the rest of Canada has generally been hostile and uncomprehending. When pushed to a justification of its refusal, it has generally taken up the language of antinationalism; indeed, it has often gone even further and rejected even (i), the whole language of identity. English Canadian spokespersons have taken refuge in the crassly philistine contention that language is just a medium of communication, that we should choose our media for greatest efficiency, and that English should therefore predominate; or else they have argued that a society needs a minimum degree of unity and this precludes allowing wide rights to all minority languages. French is assimilated, on this argument, with all the languages spoken by new Canadians, and this assimilation by itself shows a complete misunderstanding of the nationalist demands of French Canada and, latterly, Quebec.

Politically, our situation seems to be this: while the argument of (a) is generally understood to be irrelevant for Quebec (by all except the minority with an insatiable taste for self- dramatization), some form of the argument I tried to formulate in (b) is accepted by the vast majority of Quebeckers. That is, even opponents of independence and of the Parti Québécois accept some moderate variant of (ii) – that language and the linguistic community form a crucial part of the horizon that defines their identity. They are not willing to sacrifice everything to it, as are the ultranationalists, but its place cannot be denied. A stand like this is almost inevitable on the part of a small people whose language and culture have been so beleaguered for so long. The alternative would have been a most stultifying fatalism.

It is because of this identification that one can speak of a French Canadian nation and, latterly, a Quebec nation. Nations exist not just where there is the objective fact of speaking the same language and sharing a common history, but where this is subjectively reflected in a people's identifications. To parody Marxist jargon, nations cannot only be *an sich*, they must also be *für sich*. Hence, almost all Quebeckers support conclusion (v) in some form. Their argument is over what the conditions are for the linguistic community's being a viable pole of identification. Does this require sovereignty? Certainly it requires some kind of political personality for Quebec. This, argue federalists, Quebec already possesses as a province in the Canadian federation.

It seems that two things prevent this being a satisfactory answer for most Quebeckers. In the first place, it is not clear that the province has all the powers it would need to ensure the level of realization it aspires to; secondly, the French fact in Canada still lacks international recognition. Sovereignty association claims to fill these two lacunae. Whether it could really deliver as promised is a big question, but, on the face of it, at least it looks as if it could. A new form of Canadian federation could do so too, one founded on a recognition of the duality that is basic to the country. A public acceptance that the country is the locus of two nations could allow the international recognition that has hitherto always been muted.

I cannot hide the fact that I consider the federal solution to be the preferable one. Sovereignty association seems to me near-disastrous for two reasons. First, there will in fact be too much divergence of interest (coupled with bad blood) for it to work. If it gets off the ground at all, it will start breaking up almost immediately, especially as the will to make it work is absent among ultranationalists in Quebec, for whom sovereignty association is only a stopgap measure to make separation less abrupt and traumatic, and thus to make it salable to the majority in the province. Even if it does get off the drawing board, sovereignty association will almost surely end badly. In the second place, sovereignty association is the project of the ultranationalists. If it wins, their vision of Quebec will be correspondingly strengthened. But few things are more spiritually destructive to a community than when ultranationalism wins out and a full-blooded affirmation of (ii) in its most extreme variant is made the basis of its social life. Not only does this breed a willingness to sacrifice everything else on the altar of the nation, but nationalism itself becomes an obsession with power. As things stand, only a renewed federation based on duality can be a long-term alternative to separation; that is, no long-term solution will be viable which fails to come to terms with the place that variants of argument (b) have in Quebec. But such a solution would require that English Canada come to have some understanding for (b) and hence for Quebec.

I have been discussing why nations have to become states. We have seen that beyond the traditional justification (a), there is a possible complex of arguments adumbrated in (b) which can justify statehood. But whereas (a) seems to give sufficient grounds for demanding sovereignty, since this is the necessary condition of republican self-rule, the predicament defined by (b) is more complicated.

The requirements of expression, realization, and recognition may push us towards sovereignty as a solution. But there may also be good reasons pushing us the other way. The advantages of supranational collaboration are more and more evident to us. These are partly economic and technological, as has been stressed in the European Community and in some of the arguments for maintaining Canadian unity. But they are also spiritual, in opening not only a wider identification but also a plurality of poles of identification. This can help protect us from the stultifying, repressive obsession with the nation, which is one of the standing dangers in modern civilization. That is why federation remains an important option, just as Montesquieu and Rousseau saw two centuries ago, when our modern ideal of self-rule began to establish itself. In the best of all worlds, nations would not have to become states. It should be one of their options (self-determination) but not the top option. A higher aspiration is supranational unity, following the best of the modern political tradition.

Notes

1 For example, Jean-Pierre Charbonneau and Gilbert Paquette, "L'Acte de 1867, une constitution colonialiste," in L'Option (Montreal: Editions de l'homme, 1978), 125.

CHAPTER FOUR

Alternative Futures:
Legitimacy, Identity, and Alienation
in Late-Twentieth-Century Canada

Because Charles Taylor in his philosophical progression is first and foremost interested in the dilemmas of modernity – in the diversity and paradoxes of the quest for identity inherent in it – his view of the Canada-Quebec crisis gains much in originality. This chapter, which was first published in 1985, carried within itself the seeds of works that reached their logical outcome in Taylor's *Sources of the Self* (Cambridge, Mass.: Harvard University Press, 1989) and his *Malaise of Modernity* (Toronto: Anansi, 1991). This study was carried out within the overarching framework of the research program of the Royal Commission on the Economic Union and Development Prospects for Canada, chaired by Donald Macdonald. There are various ways of responding to the phenomena of growth, concentration, and mobility that arise in modern societies. After vividly sketching the malaise of modernity, Taylor here explores the choices open to Canada. According to him, Canadians must remember, before acting, that they cannot count on consensus with regard to national identity.

THE MALAISE OF MODERNITY

CONTEMPORARY SOCIETY SUFFERS FROM a certain malaise of impending breakdown. This is not to say that we all worry about this all the

Taken from *Constitutionalism, Citizenship, and Society in Canada*, ed. Alan Cairns and Cynthia Williams (Toronto: University of Toronto Press, 1985). Reprinted by permission of University of Toronto Press Incorporated in co-operation with the Royal Commission on the Economic Union and Development Prospects for Canada and the Canadian Government Publishing Centre: Study 33.

time. On the contrary, we are often unbearably smug, particularly in this country. But from time to time, when some new dislocation looms or tension rises, the fear surfaces of a collapse in our political or legal order, betokening at best a dissolution of our polity, and perhaps even removing our safeguards against a condition of arbitrary violence and despotism of which each day's international news offers us vivid images from less fortunate parts of the globe.

What else is new? All societies at all times have suffered from such fears. In the case of all previously existing civilizations, not without reason, for they all ultimately did break down. What is special about our case is that we see the breakdown coming about in a particular way. We see it coming through hypertrophy, through our becoming too much what we have been. This kind of fear is perhaps definitive of the modern age, the fear that the very things that define our break with earlier "traditional" societies – our affirmation of freedom, equality, radical new beginnings, control over nature, democratic self-rule – will somehow be carried beyond feasible limits and will undo us. The hard-boiled optimist will perhaps see this fear as a relic of atavistic beliefs in divine nemesis as an answer to our hubris, but it is hard to conjure it away altogether in this fashion.

Various theories of modernity cast this fear of hypertrophy in different forms. According to some, modern society risks breakdown through the loss of meaning. What defines the modern break is the rejection of the sense, seemingly universal among pre-moderns, that human beings and their societies were set in a broader cosmic order which determined their paradigm purposes and defined what the good was for them. Our modern idea of the free, self-defining subject is of an agent who finds his paradigm purposes in himself and can legitimately have them defined for him by a larger order only if he has consented to this subordination. The social contract theories of the seventeenth century embed this new understanding of the subject.

One form that the fear of breakdown takes is the sense that the rejection of all such encompassing orders must also put an end to all horizons of meaning. The ideally free agent faces total emptiness, in which nothing can be recognized any more as of intrinsic worth. The ultimate viability of all horizons rested on the sense of being embedded in an order. For a time, there can be a purpose to human life in the liberation from this, but once the destructive task is completed, no positive purpose remains. A threat of this kind seems to be proffered in the famous Nietzschean image of the death of God. Another form of this fear surfaces in the work of Max Weber, who was deeply influenced by Nietzsche. Modern political life needs ever new doses of charismatic leadership in order to stave off a kind of emptiness and imprisonment in the routine.

In this version of the fear of hypertrophy, modern freedom undermines itself by destroying meaning. But there are other versions of the hypertrophy fear in which the very excesses of modern freedom and equality lead directly to self-destruction. In one variant of these, the modern exaltation of individual freedom ends up eroding the loyalties and allegiances to the wider community which any society needs to survive. This danger was first articulated in the period of the Restoration in France and was the starting point for the reflections of Tocqueville, who tried to determine how this consequence of modernity could be avoided, how indeed the Anglo-Saxon societies seemed at least provisionally to have avoided it. In a slightly different variant, influentially articulated by Burke, it is the modern aspiration to negate history and to create social structures from scratch, which has fateful and ineluctable self-destructive consequences.

According to another version again, it is not so much the hypertrophy of individual freedom but the insistence on political equality and mass participation that puts impossible demands on modern societies and leads to their downfall. The theorists of a revised, elite theory of democracy, who wrote in the wake of Schumpeter after World War II, entertained a view of this sort.[1] In the 1970s a new wave of theories arose whose purport was that modern democratic states were becoming "ungovernable," partly because of an overload of subjective demands, but also because the tasks of government in a contemporary technological-industrial society tend to escalate beyond its means.[2]

A rather different variant of the modern fear, which also stems from Weber, is the notion that capitalism, or modern industrial society, while depending on a certain ethic of austere self-discipline (the famous "Protestant ethic"), inevitably undermines this ethic by its very productive success and by fostering an outlook of hedonism and self-gratification that undermines the very success that gave rise to it. Daniel Bell has presented a view of this kind in his *Cultural Contradictions of Capitalism*.[3]

One of the most widely canvassed hypertrophy stories in our time is that propounded by the ecological movements – that modern society is in danger of destroying itself through its commitment to headlong growth. I will return to this critique in greater detail below. The idea that modern society is bent on self-destruction through an excess of its own essential qualities is not necessarily pessimistic. Marxism presents a view of this kind about capitalism in which the outcome is for the best. The breakdown allows for a higher, socialist organization of society in which the good qualities of modern civilization are at last integrally rescued and made compatible. But towards the end of the twentieth century it is hard for anyone, socialist or conservative, to look on breakdown with this kind of optimism. Almost no one can believe that a solution to the modern dilemma might be achieved just by the collapse of capitalism. And so the hypertrophy fear tends to haunt everyone, left and right.

Framing the fear of breakdown in terms of hypertrophy tends to suggest the idea that the most successful modern societies are those that have an admixture of the traditional, those that somehow avoid going too far down the road to modernity. There is a long tradition of comment on British democracy based on this theme – that the genius (or good luck) of British democracy lies simply in the welding of highly traditional elements, rooted in earlier centuries, with the modern aspirations to freedom, equality, and democracy. The formula for survival in this view is modernity only in moderate doses. Another very common notion, which accompanies this, is of the view of recent centuries as a march through modernity into the postmodern danger zone of hypertrophy. In this image, some societies are ahead of others and presage the possible future fate of these others. The United States today (in particular certain parts of it, such as California) is cast in this role. This view sees the formula for survival as having modernity occur as slowly as possible.

These two views – moderation or slowness as the key to survival – offer satisfaction and assurance to Canadians. We have a commonly established self-image of being more rooted in the past than American civilization, with part of our society steeped in the British tradition (stemming from the Loyalists who refused the American Revolution), and stemming from a French community cut off from the mother country before the revolution. The very sense that we are "behind" the Americans can also be a source of reassurance and superiority when we think of the threatened rush of modernity into breakdown. These images provide the basis for a certain Canadian smugness, which perhaps compensates for what we sometimes see as a certain unimaginative stodginess in the national character.

But perhaps this way of conceiving the danger in terms of "too much" or "too fast" is wrong. Or perhaps, to give it its due, it is close enough in certain respects to function as a tolerable first approximation, but fails to give real insight into the processes of modernity and the threats it can pose. This I believe to be the case. The straight hypertrophy story is too crude, because it understands the goods which have allegedly overgrown their limits – freedom, equality, technological control – from the outside only. Perhaps a finer-grained understanding of what they mean to moderns will put the issue in a quite different light. It will no longer just be a question of whether we have gained too much of them too fast; rather, the difference between survival and breakdown may be seen to turn on our ability to realize these goods in an authentic form. Our agenda will then no longer be defined as limiting or slowing down the progress of modern values, but rather as finding a way to rescue them in their integrity, as against the distortions and perversions that have developed in modern history.

These two conceptions and their corresponding agendas – of limitation and rescue, respectively – belong to outlooks which one might describe as pessimistic and optimistic, and to some extent line up with policies which might be defined as conservative and reform, respectively.[4] I do not want to prejudge which of these approaches is right in this study, although I must admit that I belong to the second, or "rescue," party. But I think that the issue cannot be properly joined until one abandons the merely external approach of most limitation theories and tries to define in a closer-grained fashion the understandings of the human good that have grown along with and underpinned the development of modern society.

This is what I intended to do first in this chapter. My belief is that it is only against this background that we can fruitfully pose questions about the causes of (and potential cures for) breakdown, both in general and in the particular case of this country. So before considering the alternative futures that may lie before us in Canada, I want to attempt to define some relevant features of the spiritual climate of modern societies. Before embarking on this, I have a few preliminary remarks that will serve to define my question more clearly.

The danger of breakdown in modern societies can be understood in terms of another central Weberian concept, that of "legitimacy." This term is meant to designate the beliefs and attitudes that members have towards the society they make up. The society has legitimacy when members so understand and value it that they are willing to assume the disciplines and burdens which membership entails. Legitimacy declines when this willingness flags or fails. Using the term in this sense, we could say that the danger of breakdown arises for us in the form of a legitimation crisis.

Of course, there are other kinds of possible dangers that arise from hypertrophy of modern development. Certain unintended negative consequences of scale, for instance, can create severe strain, such as the sclerosis that might arise from large-scale bureaucratization, or the notorious pollution effects of certain kinds of economic growth, or the skewed economic priorities which some allege to be the inevitable outcome of uncontrolled free-enterprise capitalism. But severe as they may be, they could not by themselves bring about a breakdown in our political or legal order; or rather, they would do so only through their effect on the legitimacy of this order. Bureaucratic sclerosis is a threat to our political order, for instance, just because this order is self-professedly democratic. A process that makes it less and less possible for people to make effective decisions about their lives threatens to bring society into conflict with its central justifying principles, and this cannot but bring about a loss of legitimacy.

The focus on legitimacy is especially relevant for modern societies. This is not because all societies at all times have not required legitimacy in this sense. But two things mark modern societies. The first is that an important part of the background out of which they arose was that legitimacy became a central philosophical problem. Underlying Weberian "legitimacy" is the seventeenth century use of the term, not to describe people's attitudes but as a term of objective evaluation of regimes. Modern political theory is inaugurated in the seventeenth century around this central question of the conditions of legitimate rule.

The second reason why legitimacy is of particular importance in modern society is that the participation demands of this society are greater in two respects than previous ones. First of all, modern industrial society is not only the fruit of an unprecedented degree of disciplined, dedicated, innovative productive activity; by an understandable reverse process, it comes to demand this kind of effort of its members. Firms operate in competition with each other, but so do all contemporary industrial societies. Any failure in that constellation of qualities that make for high productivity – which certainly includes a certain attitude towards work and certain patterns of investment – and the less competitive economy is threatened with relative de-industrialization and hence higher unemployment, slower growth, relative impoverishment, and all that goes with this. Contemporary societies cannot afford not to take production seriously – or rather, the costs of not doing so can be very high. Certainly some societies, like contemporary Britain, seem willing to pay these costs up to a point. But presumably, even Britons would consider some level of relative impoverishment too high, and at that point would feel the full weight of competitive demand. The second respect in which modern societies are more demanding is that, at least in the First World (Western societies plus Japan), they tend to be liberal democracies. This means that they are based on the principles of political participation, self-voted taxation burdens, the citizen army as the ultimate instrument of defence, and the like. As I argue below, this aspect of modern societies as self-governing is of central significance to the understanding of the good that is constitutive of modern society.

In these two respects, we can see why the modern problem of legitimacy has peculiar significance for modern society. If we define this in terms of the attitudes and beliefs of members which dispose them to assume or refuse to assume the disciplines and burdens of membership in a given society, we can understand how as legitimacy increases in importance, the more weighty are the disciplines and burdens that must be voluntarily assumed. For the ideal despotism, legitimacy carries a much lesser weight, at least until that point where oppression drives the subjects to revolt. But in contemporary industrial democracies, the everyday operations must call on an ever-present fund of positive identification.

This provides the background to the contemporary concern with legitimacy and to fears of a "legitimation crisis."[5] But how can we get an intellectual grip on this? One very simple way would be to see legitimacy as a function of satisfaction, defined in relatively tough-minded terms – for example, those of economic living standards (in relation perhaps to expectations). In this view, a regime gains or loses legitimacy as it delivers or fails to deliver the goods. This would make our problem easier; and certainly no one can deny that economic satisfaction is one important factor in the survival and breakdown of political regimes. But it is obvious, too, that it is absurdly one-sided to consider this alone.

If we want to go deeper into the bases for legitimacy and its loss, we have to understand more about the conceptions of the good life, the notions of human fulfilment, of human excellence and its potential distortion, which have grown up along with modern society. We need that finer-grained understanding noted above, an understanding of the notions that have framed the identity of our contemporaries.

When I speak of notions of the good that have grown up with modern society, I do not refer to some merely accidental correlation. Rather, I mean the understandings of the good that have helped constitute this society and hence are essentially linked to its development. These conceptions, which I gather together under the loose title of the modern identity, could only have developed within a society with structures, institutions, and practices like ours. Take, for example, our widespread conception of ourselves as autonomous individuals, choosing our own values and modes of life. This self-interpretation, and hence ideal, is not one that any one of us could have invented and sustained alone, in the midst, say, of a closed tribal society. It is one that is available for us because we live in a civilization where this conception has been formulated and defined. What is more, it is available to us because we live in a civilization in which this conception underlies many social practices.

For instance, we cast votes as individuals to reach social decisions; that is, we vote in isolation in a polling booth, and not in the sight of all in the ecclesia. We are expected to formulate our individual opinions and outlook, to arrive at them on our own, to take responsibility for them. Pollsters are constantly sampling for our individual opinions. Or again, we have a common practice of negotiation in which individuals or parties define their goals quite independently of the rest of society and then try to reach some agreed ground. Many of the ground rules that hold our institutions together are based on such contracts. We even have been induced to believe at various times that the most basic and ultimate framework, the political, was or ought to be established by contract. Or again, in our society the family is based on the freely chosen companionate marriage; you choose a partner according to your own affinities.

All these practices and institutions induce us to understand ourselves as individuals; more, they make it inevitable that we do so. I have my opinions, my values, my outlook, my affinities. We have developed in this direction to a degree unprecedented in history; some of our self-attributions would be shocking or even incomprehensible to our ancestors. What would a medieval or any but a few sophists among the ancients make of "my values"? The very word "value" belongs to our "subjectivist" civilization. None of us except a tiny number gifted with imaginative genius could have stepped out of that medieval or ancient outlook into our contemporary one. If what was incomprehensible to them seems self-evident to us, it is because we live in a civilization in which practices like the above are dominant.

The relation between practices and conceptions can be put in this way: the notion of myself as an individual is constitutive of these practices, is presupposed in them. A social practice is a rule or norm-governed activity. It is defined by certain norms of failure and success, of honesty and turpitude, of excellence or mediocrity, and so on. A certain conception of the human person is presupposed in a practice if it is essential to understanding the norms which define it. But the norms defining modern citizen voting, or the companionate marriage, presuppose the autonomous individual. It is an infringement if someone else can oversee my vote, because I must be free of any intimidation and vote according to my own conscience. I am expected to marry someone I love; caving in to my extended family or to social expectation is a falling off, and acquiescence in the second best.

This relation of presupposition is directly relevant to legitimacy. Institutions are defined by certain norms and constituted by certain normative conceptions of man. It is these conceptions that they sustain. But the relationship of support also works the other way. It is these normative conceptions that give the institutions their legitimacy. Should people cease to believe in them, the institutions would infallibly decay; they could no longer command the allegiance of those who participate in them. Institutions demand discipline, frequently sacrifice, always at least the homage of taking their norms seriously. When they lose legitimacy, they lose these.

The question for the "internal" perspective is this: on a proper understanding of the modern identity – the set of conceptions of man that has grown with modern society, constitutive of its institutions and practices – has the development of these structures, institutions, and practices tended to their own undermining, either by shaking men's faith in their constitutive norms or by making these practices and institutions appear as perversions of these norms? I think that in fact something of this kind has been and is now taking place, and that is why an exploration of the modern identity can help us to understand our contemporary legitimation crisis, and perhaps to arbitrate between the optimistic and pessimistic, the "rescue" and "limitation" perspectives adumbrated above.

STRAINS OF THE MODERN IDENTITY

I want to turn now to that family of conceptions of human beings, of freedom, and of human nature which emerge roughly in the seventeenth century and which have been woven into our developing commercial and later industrial capitalist society. It is these concepts that I refer to collectively as the "modern identity." Two phases in its development continue to exert a strong influence in our time.

One of the key notions of the first phase was the new conceptions of freedom that emerged in the seventeenth century. This period saw a progressive rejection of world views in which humans were seen as forming part of some cosmic order, where their nature was to be understood by their relation to that order. Both the new conceptions of science and the new notion of autonomy pointed to a view of humans as beings who discover their purposes in themselves. "Nature" becomes internalized in the modern period. In this view, the free subject becomes someone who follows an internal purpose and who owes no a priori allegiance to a pre-existing order but gives it only to structures that were created by his or her own consent. Even the ancient conceptions of the freedom of the citizen, which were essentially defined as a certain relation to a whole – the polis or republic – go into eclipse, and we find atomist conceptions of freedom developing where persons are seen to enjoy "natural liberty" in a state of nature.

Along with this notion of freedom comes a new conception of what human nature demands. Traditional moral views grounded on nature, which descend from the ancients, offer what we might call a two-tiered view of the good life. This consists primarily in some higher activity distinct from the fulfilment of ordinary needs involved with the production and reproduction of life. Meeting these ordinary needs is of course unavoidable and good but is regarded simply as infrastructural to a distinct activity that gives life its higher significance. In one version this was defined as contemplation; in another influential version, as the life of the citizen. In either version, lives that lacked the favoured activity and were entirely absorbed in meeting life needs were regarded as truncated and deprived. It followed that outside of very exceptional social contexts, the fullness of human life was only for the few.

To some extent Christianity worked against these aristocratic conceptions, but the Christian church too developed a notion of an exceptional vocation higher than that of the ordinary person, which was associated with celibacy. One of the central tenets of the Reformation was the rejection of this notion of the special vocation and the preaching of a vision of ordinary life as hallowed. A secularized version of this arises in the seventeenth century.

The demands of nature, of the new internalized nature, just are the ordinary needs of life. There is no higher stratum of activity. Rather, what defines proper human activity is a certain manner of going about meeting these needs – in a sober, disciplined, clair-voyant, and rational way. This last term, "rationality," could be taken to sum up the properly human way of living. But it now, of course, changes its sense. It is defined less and less in terms of a vision of the true order of things and more and more in terms of instrumental reason. The rational pursuit of the needs of life crucially includes seeking them in an effective manner.

The ethic that rejects a class distinction in purposes and activities is also anti-aristocratic in social thrust. The norm of rational pursuit of ordinary life needs is, in a sense, the bourgeois ethic. An example of the remarkable penetration of this ethos into our whole civilization is the development of the modern notion of the family. From the seventeenth century on, in the higher classes of Anglo-Saxon societies and spreading outward and downward from these, we find a new outlook in which the companionate marriage and the life of the nuclear family come more and more to be seen as one of the central fulfilments of human life. This has become so much a part of our contemporary world that we find it hard to imagine a time when it was not so. But it is relatively recent in human history. The modern need for privacy is part of this same development, as is the growing emphasis on sentiment. One of the ways of understanding modern consumer society is as an attempt to make available for the vast majority the conditions of self-enclosed family life as this ideal has developed in the past three centuries.[6] A second facet of this outlook has been the extraordinary development of forms of mass discipline – the reg-imenting of gesture and action to produce maximum effect – which begins in the eighteenth century in armies, schools, prisons, factories, and so on. This has been interestingly traced by Michel Foucault in his *Surveiller et punir*.[7]

In connection with this last phenomenon, we can see a third leading notion developing in this period which I call "efficacy." The free individual meeting the demands of nature in the modern sense must aspire to a higher degree of control over himself and over nature. Exercising the control that enables one to effect one's purposes more fully and to a higher degree is a mark of rationality

– that is, one is pursuing one's life needs in a properly human way.

The modern identity can be sketchily characterized, I believe, in terms of these three notions – liberty, nature, and efficacy. They characterize what I call phase one. But there is another version of this identity which emerges in the late eighteenth century, partly in reaction to phase one. It is what we see in various forms in Rousseau, in Romanticism, and to some degree also in certain religious movements – arguably, for instance, in Methodism. Its secular variant can perhaps be identified as an alternative reading of the modern notion of life according to nature. In phase one, the rejection of aristocratic ethics takes place in favour of an ideal of the pursuit of ordinary purposes under rational control. The purposes themselves are not endowed with special significance. What is quintessentially human is the rational control. But for the new counter-tradition, the rejection of supposed higher activities means rather that our ordinary purposes are endowed with higher significance. To fulfil the true impulse of nature in us is not just to meet a biological need but also to satisfy a higher aspiration. It is, at the same time, a moral fulfilment. From Rousseau on, the true "voice of nature" is at the same time both the impulse of biological need and an aspiration to what is experienced as moral self-realization.

From this perspective the modern notion of life according to nature involves a fusion of the biological and the moral instead of their hierarchical ordering as with traditional moralities, or their setting in a relation of rational control as in the first form of the modern identity. This has been a tremendously influential idea in the last two centuries of modern culture, well beyond the epoch of Rousseau or the Romantics. Indeed, I would argue that it is central to the Marxist aspiration to a condition in which individuals would be creative (in the artistic sense) in their productive life. Closing the gap between creativity and production is another variant of this fused perspective.

This view has been the basis for many of the criticisms of modern industrial society, even as the first phase has provided much of the justification for it. For the fused perspective is naturally highly critical of the primacy accorded to instrumental reason, which must presuppose that ends were given independently of reason and which tends to make us look at nature merely as a set of obstacles or instruments for our purposes. But however critical of the first phase, this second phase is recognizably a variant of the modern identity. It grows unquestionably out of the modern notion of the internalization of nature, and it develops its own conceptions of freedom as the following of autonomously generated purposes. However much they come in conflict, these two variants cannot wholly repudiate each other, and this fact is reflected in the complexity of their relations in modern culture.

This conception of life according to nature, in its two versions, has grown up with modern society. It has been embedded in the structures, practices, and institutions of this society – in our relations of production; in our application of technology to production on a massive scale; in our sexual relations and family forms; in our political institutions and practices. Some of these institutions and practices have been of crucial importance in sustaining this modern identity. This has generally been lost sight of because the modern identity itself (in phase one) has stressed individual autonomy to the point where the necessity of social mediation has been lost. The modern identity has too easily bred myths of social contract – and is still doing so today in a transposed way.[8]

But we can single out several features of modern society that have played a vital part in developing and sustaining our sense of ourselves as free agents. The first is equality. Clearly, the modern identity is incompatible with the status of serf or slave. However, the requirement is stronger than this. The identity of the free subject establishes a strong presumption in favour of equality. In contrast, hierarchical societies are justified on the old conception of a cosmic logos. Different groups are seen as expressing complementary principles. This has been the traditional justification of hierarchy everywhere – different classes and functions correspond to different links in the chain of being. Each is necessary for the other and for the whole, and the place of each relative to the others is thus natural, right, and according to the order of things. Once this view is swept aside, the basic justification of hierarchy disappears. All self-determining subjects are alike in this crucial respect. There is no further valid ground for hierarchy as an unquestionable unchanging order of precedence.

Equality is thus one dimension of the free subject's relation to society. Another very obtrusive dimension is that one must be the subject of rights. As a free subject, one is owed respect for one's rights and has certain guaranteed freedoms. One must be able to choose and act, within limits, free from the arbitrary interference of others. The modern subject is an equal bearer of rights. This status is part of what sustains the subject's identity.

Perhaps these two conditions express the basic minimum status of a modern subject in society without which identity must founder or the predicament is experienced as intolerable. But there have been other important features of this status which are worth mentioning. One of the most important faculties of the modern subject is the ability to effect one's purposes. This is what I have called "efficacy." Subjects without efficacy, unable to alter the world around them to their ends, would either be incapable of sustaining a modern identity or would be deeply humiliated in their identity. To a considerable degree, each of us can have a sense of efficacy in our own individual action – getting the means to live, providing for the family, acquiring goods, going about our business, and so on. The very fact that we command so much private space is important for our sense of efficacy. For example, the ability a car gives one to move around on one's own gives many people the sense of power, of efficacy, of being able to do things and to get to places on their own, and also has affinities with a sense of sexual potency. But important as private efficacy is, it is not possible to make it the whole, to give no thought at all to one's efficacy as a member of society, affecting its direction or having a part in the global efficacy that society possesses relative to nature.

Thus, along with the sense of having equal rights, there are two other important features of our status in society which have played a role in sustaining the modern identity. The first is our status as citizens, in terms of which we collectively determine the course of social events. The modern West has taken up this ancient tradition – that only citizens are full persons capable of acting and making a name for themselves in human memory – and has made this an integral part of our sense of efficacy. The fact that we govern ourselves is an extremely important part of our dignity as free subjects.

The second dimension is that of production. As producers, in the broadest sense, we belong to a whole interconnected society of labour and technology which has immense efficacy in transforming nature and produces more astonishing wonders every day. Insofar as we belong to this society, work in it, take part in it, contribute to it, we have a share in this efficacy. We can think of it as partly ours, as a confirmation of ourselves. This is an important part of our sense of what we are in an advanced industrial society. It is also an important source of malaise and of a creeping sense of unavoidable inferiority among Third World elites.

The modern subject, therefore, is far from being an independent, atomic agent. One may be so relative to the local community, but one cannot be so relative to the whole society. On the contrary, an individual is sustained, on one hand, by the culture which elaborates and maintains the vocabulary of his or her self-understanding and, on the other, by the society in which he or she has a status commensurate with free subjectivity – a status in which we have isolated four dimensions of the equal bearer of rights who is producer and citizen. All of this underpins one's identity as a free individual who could not long survive a state of nature.

The set of practices by which the society defines my status as an equal bearer of rights, an economic agent, and a citizen – practices such as the operation of the legal system, the political system of voting and elections, the practices of negotiation and collective bargaining – all have embedded in them a conception of the agent and his or her relation to society which reflects the modern identity and its related visions of the good. The growth of this identity can help to explain why these practices have developed in the direction they have – why, for instance, voting and collective adversary negotiation take a bigger and bigger place in our societies. But it may also help to explain why we experience a growing malaise today.

It is perhaps not hard to see how our contemporary society satisfies the modern identity. The first phase of the modern identity stressed three things: autonomy, fulfilment of our nature, and efficacy, the last being a confirmation of our control, our productive power, and hence our freedom from things. Modern consumer society satisfies these three demands, or appears to. It affords privacy, treats us as autonomous beings who are efficacious as producers and citizens, and seems aimed towards providing us with a sense of fulfilment which we determine along with those with whom we have knit ties of intimacy. It also appears to satisfy some of the variants of natural fulfilment of the second version – particularly the Romantic-expressive ones – since much of our private fulfilment in our relationships and in our artistic and expressive life is drawn from expressive models. In a sense, we are Romantics in our private existence – our love lives are drawn by a notion of Romantic mutual discovery. We look for fulfilments in our hobbies and in our recreation, while the economic, legal, and political structures in which we coexist are largely justified instrumentally.

But then this compromise between phases one and two, which at times seems so stable, at other times seems racked with tension. Now is one of those times. We can also understand some of the background for this. We have seen how phase two of our ideal of natural fulfilment can be turned into a powerful critique of the first version. So we immediately understand the strictures which are flung at our political, economic, and legal structures – that they are merely instrumental, that they deny community, that they are exploitative of humans and nature, and so on. In this we can see how closely interwoven both the affirmative and critical stances are to our contemporary society, how much they are from the same roots and draw on the same sources. But perhaps we can also hope to gain some insight into the dialectic between the two, how the balance tips now one way, now another.

What the efficacious industrial consumer society has going for it is, presumably, that it delivers the goods. But if we examine this society in the light of the modern identity, we can see that this achievement is not just a matter of meeting quantitative targets. Rather, we see that, in phase one, efficacy is valued as the fruit and sign of rational control. Increasing production originally became a value in our civilization, against all the temptations to sloth and all the blandishments of traditional ethics, because in producing we came to see ourselves as not just meeting our needs but also as realizing our status as autonomous, rational agents. Continued accumulation bespoke a consistent, disciplined main-tenance of the instrumental stance to things; it was a realization of our spiritual dimension. Far from being an obsession with things or an entrapment in them, as it might be stigmatized in a Platonic conception, it is an affirmation of our autonomy in that our purposes are not imposed on us by the supposed order of things. The instrumental stance towards nature is meant to be a spiritual declaration of independence from it.

From this we can understand the potential vulnerability of this kind of society and way of life. The ways and forms of its accumulation have to go on appearing as affirmations of freedom and efficacy. Should they be seen as degenerating into mere self-indulgence, then the society undergoes a crisis of confidence. This is a moral crisis but one that is also inescapably a political crisis. For what is impugned is the definition of the good actually embedded in our practices. Should we come to repudiate this, our allegiance to these practices and therefore our society itself is threatened. Thus, it follows that our society has always been vulnerable to a certain moral critique. It is in trouble if it stands self-convicted, in the eyes of its members, of pure materialism – that is, of aiming purely at material enrichment. This may not be evident because of certain commonplaces of sociological comment such as that which alleges we are more hedonistic in outlook than our ancestors.[9]

There are some ways in which this is true, but it does not make any less important the underlying sense that our dignity consists in our capacity to dominate things and not to be dominated by them. For this is rooted in the modern identity. If more people are willing to accept a "permissive" society today, it is because they see that such self-indulgence can be combined with the free self-direction whereby we determine our own purpose and fulfilment. In this they lean partly on ceratin post-Romantic notions of emotional fulfilment. Those who find this combination hard to accept are precisely those who are most worried and rendered most anxious by the permissive society. Even the revolutionaries who call for a total rejection of the work discipline of the "Protestant ethic" can do so because of a conception of freedom which is allegedly the fruit of such total abandonment. That this is not realistic should not blind us to the kind of hope it is – one still very much in line with modern identity.

Indeed, one could argue that the more a society is founded on the modern ideal of life according to nature in its first version, the more it should be vulnerable to doubts about its moral standing and the more these doubts will be unsettling. It is not surprising to find that this kind of worry is a very old one in the United States. Fred Somkin[10] has shown how the prosperity of the republic in the early nineteenth century raised soul searchings. On the one hand, it was just what one might expect – a proof of efficacy and, hence, of the spiritual excellence of America. On the other hand, it seemed to threaten vice, self-indulgence, a forgetfulness of republican virtue, and the demands of the spirit. As Somkin showed, it was essential for many Americans of the time to prove that prosperity was indeed a fruit of the spirit. The alternative was too unsettling to contemplate.

My claim is that we have not left behind the era when we could be shaken by this kind of doubt. It is not a relic of an earlier "puritan" era. In a transposed way, many of the features of the puritan era have been recreated in our contemporary variant of the modern identity, but now the relevance of this has spread well beyond the United States and beyond the Anglo-Saxon world. Many societies have been made over so that their dominant practices, not only of economic and public life but also family life, reflect the modern identity. With this in mind, let us look at the features of contemporary society which tend to undermine our confidence in it as moderns.

The first of these is alienation at work. For a great many people, work is dull, monotonous, without meaning, and "soul-destroying," to use Schumacher's word.[11] Connected with this is the fact that, in work relations, most individuals are far from the equal, autonomous subjects that they are at home or feel themselves to be as consumers. For the most part, they stand very much as subordinates in command relations and have very little say about how they will work or in what conditions.

We enter here onto Marx's terrain. It is impossible to make a sensible critique of consumer society without invoking Marx. But there is one very important amendment that I want to make at the outset. I want to see the present formula of consumer society, with its mix of fulfilment and distortion, as a kind of historic

compromise in which most of us have acquiesced. Orthodox Marxists, however, are committed to seeing it as an alienating (provided
they want to use this word) formula imposed on the working
masses by the ruling class through a mixture of force, mendacious
persuasion, propaganda, control of information, divisive tactics,
and so on. But this seems to me very wrong. The working class
of early industrial society was certainly pitched into the proletarian
role against its will, with terrible conditions of sweated labour and
blighted townscape, and was held in place by force where it tried
to resist. But in the one hundred and fifty years since then, our
societies have become mass democracies. Work conditions under
capitalism have been profoundly modified, workers receive much
greater remuneration, and they have substantial control over conditions through trade unions and political power.

It is difficult to argue that what remains unmodified in capitalism remains so because of force and fraud when so much else
has been changed, often against the better resistance of industri-
alists. Rather, the compromise of affluent society must be seen to
represent a tacit acquiescence – for the present, anyway – in subordinate relations of labour on the part of the mass of workers. It
consists of accepting alienated labour in return for consumer affluence. This compromise can seem to make sense in the lives of
many people in part because this alienation can be represented as
the necessary condition of affluence: by not demanding citizenship
in the workplace, the worker allows the provident engine of
industry to run untrammelled and generate ever-growing prosperity. But the compromise can also be appealing because alienation is the obverse of non-involvement, the condition of complete
mobility. To become a citizen at work would require some commitment to the enterprise and the devotion of some of the worker's
life energies to this community and its plans and decisions. Otherwise, the participation becomes a mere sham or the manipulated
instrument of active minorities. But this devotion is a price that
the aspiring consumer-citizen may be unwilling to pay – a limitation on the self-contained life. The development of the affluent
society, in which the majority can preside over a self-contained
life in adequate private space, has thus gone along with a tacit
reluctance to challenge the regime of alienated, subordinate labour.
This is the first distortion. The fact that it is connived in by the

majority, rather than being brutally imposed on them, does not make it any more healthy.

A second compromise that must be accepted in contemporary society is lack of control over priorities. The sense of the common interest that underlies this compromise is that the machine must run on. But the machine that we find ourselves with in our societies is a capitalist one – that is, it consists mainly of enterprises whose institutional goals are to grow through the accumulation and reinvestment of profit. These enterprises have become immensely effective in some ways in the application of technology to this end. But they cannot easily tolerate interference that attempts to set priorities for the production process. A modern capitalist economy can take (indeed, requires) much intervention to keep it going – fiscal and monetary controls, subsidies of all sorts. But basic to its operation is the principle that firms must be masters of their own investment, able to invest where they can accumulate the greatest profits, foster the greatest overall growth, maintain market share most effectively, or some such objective. The condition of the machine's running effectively is that no one tries to control its priorities too closely. Thus, we get the culture that moral critics object to – the fixation on brute quantitative growth unalloyed by judgments of priority. The justification for this is an image of the good life in which the acquisition of more and more consumer goods – what the system is good at producing – is seen as a central purpose of life.

Once again, most of us acquiesced in this historic compromise for similarly mixed reasons as we did to alienated labour. On the one hand, the non-imposition of priorities seemed to be the condition of the machine's running continuously; on the other, the resultant mode of life satisfied us as modern subjects in certain ways. First, the disinvolvement, our collective silence on priorities, seemed the condition of our freedom severally to "hang loose," to build our own private spaces and live our own self-contained lives. Secondly, the definition of the good life as a continuing escalation in living standards has an inescapable appeal to unregenerated persons, which we all are. This Plato well knew. Appetite tends to run on to infinity unless controlled by reason. The consumer society appeals to the lowest in us. But this is only a half-truth. It is also the case that the consumer society comes to us dressed up in a form that meshes with some of the aspirations of the modern subject. Thus, we are invited as consumers to acquire and furnish a private space as the condition of an autonomous, self-contained, unmediated existence. We need this space so that we and our family can grow and be close to nature (a garden, a house in the country). Much advertising plays on this aspiration to private space – the ads always show happy families filling those interiors, driving away in those cars, surrounding those barbecues, and so on. Of course, what is not justified is the continued increase. Why should the mobile private space we travel in become ever more rapid and high-powered? Why must labour-saving mechanization continue without stop, even up to electric toothbrushes and similar absurdities? This could never be justified intellectually, but somehow the implication is that more and more powerful accoutrements mean more of the fulfilment that they are meant to make possible. The commodities become "fetishized" – in a non-Marxist sense, endowed magically with the properties of the life they subserve, as though a faster car might actually make my family life more intense and harmonious.

There is a third reason why this compromise appeals to us that also aids in the fetishization of commodities. The runaway machine, doing prodigies of technological mastery of nature, satisfies our sense of collective efficacy. Members of this society can feel that participative efficacy as producers that I spoke of above. At the same time, personal efficacy is a theme often played on fetishized commodities. This is what is appealing about high-powered cars and powerful engines generally. This is turn taps feelings of machismo and sexual potency. Advertisers are aware of this. Thus, we acquiesce in the consumer goods' standard of welfare. And we accept the suspension of our sense of priorities which allows us to see as normal some truly absurd inversions, such as supersonic flight, until we break the thrall and look afresh and astonished at what we are doing.

These features of industrial society – the meaninglessness and subordination of work, the mindless lack of control of priorities, and, above all, the fetishization of commodities – all represent a challenge to our image of ourselves as realized moderns determining our purposes out of ourselves, dominating and not being dominated by things. To the extent that we let these negative features impinge on our self-understanding, we cannot but feel a fading confidence, an unease, a suspicion that the continued sense of efficacy by which we sustain our self-image within the modern identity is a sham. If we see ourselves as the playthings of mindless impersonal forces, or worse, as the victims of a fascination with mere things (and this in the very practices which are supposed to sustain our identity and our conception of good), then we cannot but lose confidence in these practices. We are threatened with a kind of anomie in which we cease to believe in the norms governing our social life but have no alternative except to live by them. There is a crisis of allegiance to our society.

I believe this is part of what underlies our present malaise. In order to understand why it arises now, we have to see why these features have begun to press themselves on us in recent years. Our consumer society is in several ways the victim of its own success – this is the relative truth in the hypertrophy story – and these ways compound to put it in crisis. First, the very prosperity of this society cannot but produce doubts and hesitations around its fetishization of commodities. When the society was still struggling to make decent housing and basic consumer durables widely available, the connection of all this effort and production with the goal of securing these goods for all was clear enough. But now that most have them, efforts to achieve refinements – the introduction of higher power, more speed, new models, frills, etc. – begin to look more and more disproportionate. It is harder to believe in all this as a serious social purpose.

Of course, a substantial minority have not yet entered the affluent society. Production for them would make sense. But the continuation of the consumer boom does not seem to be very effective in helping these "pockets of poverty." Wealth does not "trickle down" very adequately. This is partly because the continued boom goes with an upping of the ante – a whole range of new products which one has to get to be well-equipped at home, in the car, and so on. Much of each year's growth is pre-empted by the already affluent, who expect a rise in their standard of living. It is very hard to prise some off to redistribute to the poor. When growth slows down or stops, as we have seen in recent years, the resistance to redistribution increases. We have only to think of the negative attitude of nearly all Western electorates to government spending, and in particular of the widespread attack on the welfare state. Canada is in fact more moderate in this regard than some other Western democracies, such as Britain and the United States, but resistance to the politics of redistribution has also had its impact there.

At the same time, the replacement of lower by higher technology can even make things worse for poorer people. It ups the cost of being poor, so to speak. One way is by making certain consumer durables essential. For example, if a society moves from the bicycle to the automobile, cities are laid out accordingly and the proximity of housing to jobs is planned on the assumption that people have cars, so it becomes necessary to have a car in order to hold a job, at least a good job, and to get around safely on city streets. Another way is by raising the cost of housing. House prices and rents are far higher in Toronto than in less developed communities such as Sydney, Nova Scotia. Growth can thus make the lot of poor people worse.

The increasingly evident fetishistic character of the consumer standard and its steady rise do not seem able to alleviate suffering where it counts or to improve what is crying out for improvement. All of this contributes to a loss of faith in the consumer standard, in the value of an indefinite increase in consumer goods and services, and in indiscriminate growth. This may affect older people less, but it visibly emerges in scepticism, questioning, and rejection by younger people.

Among the things that may be cast into doubt in this crisis is the value of family life itself. This is particularly critical, because the version of the modern identity predominant in our society is one that aims towards a mobile subject who loosens the ties of larger communities and finds himself on his own in the nuclear family. But this gives a tremendously heightened significance to the nuclear family, which is now the main locus of strong, lasting, defining relations, and it has given family life and the emotions of family love a uniquely important place in the modern conception of natural fulfilment, beginning in the eighteenth century.

For this to be challenged is thus critical for the identity which has been dominant in our society. But it is under threat not only because it is associated with a (to some) discredited consumer way of life. It is also threatened by the very scope of the development of the modern identity. In effect, if the business of life is to find my authentic fulfilment as an individual, and if my associations should be relativized to this end, in principle there seems to be no reason why this relativization should stop at the boundary of the family. If my development or even my discovery of self should be incompatible with a long-standing association, it will come to be felt as a prison rather than a locus of identity. This places marriage under great strain, which is further intensified because the same aspiration to self-development and self-fulfilment leads women today to challenge the distribution of roles and the emotional give-and-take of the traditional family.

Population concentration and mobility are other developments that are beginning to have social consequences which produce tension in our society. Beyond a certain threshold, the concentration of people in large cities begins to have negative consequences. Unless cities are well designed with multiple centres, the ordinary business of daily life becomes more time-consuming and stressful, and relations with other people become more full of tension. In addition, large cities cost more per capita to run. As Hugh Stretton puts it, "They generate more travel, congestion and local pollution per head. They force wasteful rates of demolition and rebuilding on their inner parts. Intense competition for central and accessible locations makes it harder to solve problems of density, shares of space and – above all – land prices."[12] So concentration begins to raise the overhead costs of social existence.

Concentration and mobility do this in other ways as well. The bleeding of local communities for the megalopolis forces a write-off of the excess, unused stock of housing and public capital in declining communities. The decline of the extended family means that society must pick up the pieces for the old, the abandoned, the chronically sick, and so on. In all these ways, concentrated and mobile life virtually forces an expansion of the public sector. The prevailing doctrines about the efficiency of concentration and giant organizations ensure that the state will compound the error by overbureaucratizing the public sector.

The enlarged public sector, both as cost and as bureaucracy, creates great malaise. As a cost, it forces higher taxes. But these are resisted by citizens, as we have come more and more to see ourselves as independent individuals. The link between high mobility – that is, the pattern of "hanging loose" from all partial communities – and the higher overheads of society is generally quite invisible to us. Ironically, it is just this pattern of hanging loose that makes us less capable of seeing the social costs of our way of life and makes us look on the public sector as a barely necessary evil. So as we increase the need for public sector activity, we decrease our own readiness to assume the burden. This thoroughly irrational state of affairs leads to all kinds of tensions and eruptions, of which the international surge of an aggressive "New Right" – advocating the impossible dream of a return to the negative state – is the most important consequence politically. What further justifies the revolt is the overbureaucratization of the public sector. This makes it not only unnecessarily costly but also less responsive to the public. Consequently, the process whereby we meet our needs through public mechanisms becomes even less transparent and this lack of transparency increases the alienation.

What is even worse is that the movement towards concentration and the breakup of partial communities is not entirely voluntary. Once the process goes a certain way, it acquires an élan which is sometimes hard to resist. One may want to stay in a smaller farming community but may find it impossible to function there as the services move out and concentrate in larger centres, in response to earlier movements as well as general concentration. So more and more people follow the trend, and more services move – schools, suppliers, outlets … And then more people move, and so on.

Thus three "successes," or hypertrophies, of the consumer society are bringing about increasing malaise: the very success of the growth of consumption tends to discredit the importance attached to material gains; the increasing stress on the goal of self-fulfilment tends to fragment the family, which was previously its privileged locus; and the increased concentration and mobility of our society alienates us from government. These strains also undermine that sense of our status within the larger society which is supportive of our identity. Unresponsive bureaucracies make us less sanguine, or frankly cynical, about citizenship; sometimes we even fear for our rights. The discredit of what I have termed the consumer standards – pursuing an indefinite increase in consumer goods and services – makes us feel less positive about the efficacy of the whole society in which we have a part as labourers.

The hypertrophy of this sense of collective efficacy is itself a fourth cause of malaise. As our awareness of belonging to an organized, technological, productive society grew, so did the confidence that we could solve any problem, given the will and the concentration of resources. This sense of bullish confidence probably reached its high point in the postwar period during the Kennedy era in the United States, when intelligence, good will, and organizing science were set to tackle the age-old problems of poverty, inequality, and racial alienation through programs of the New Frontier. The sense of new creation was heightened by the symbolism of an attractive young man at the head of the enterprise. Since then, however, things have gone sour. We are made more and more aware that some problems, including the most grievous social ones such as intractable poverty and racial division, resist even immense resources. They are more than problems; they are human dilemmas. The sense of our efficacy has taken a grievous blow.

In sum, by this combined effect we have been led partly to lose confidence in our definitions of the good life, partly to feel alienated from and even cynical about our governmental institutions, partly to feel uncertain and tense about our social relations and even about our family life, partly to feel unsupported by the larger society in our identity as modern subjects.

All of this is likely to make for strains, tensions, and mutual aggressiveness. As it happens, a bout of social conflict was probably coming our way after the halcyon decades of steady consumer growth in the earlier postwar period. This was partly because of the growth of the public sector and its consequent burden on the productive sector and on taxpayers. But it is also because we live in a society which has become more equal and "classless" in style and spirit, a society in which workers and the less well-off have acquired greater bargaining muscle through trade unions, in which the general standard of education has risen, and in which there is a prevailing belief that government can do anything, so the age-old poverty, or underdevelopment, or inequality, formerly seen as in the order of things, is now removable. Such a society will sooner or later make demands on government and the economy which by their very nature and number will be incompatible.

To face this, a society needs an even higher degree of cohesion, self-confidence, and mechanisms of effective self-management. Instead, we have confronted this period with lower confidence, more inner tensions, and greater alienation from our institutions than before. The result has been a scramble for income and advantage in which powerful forces struggle to compete and maintain their position, but at the expense of the unorganized through inflation. We are being forced to return to more orderly consensus through the disastrous experience of inflation. But it is a slow and reluctant business and leaves many burning resentments and senses of grievance without vent, because we are being forced to decide about things that had previously been allowed to happen without planning, such as the distribution of income. We are being forced to take a greater hand in the collective direction of our economy. But agreement on this, hard enough at any time, is possible only with some sense of purpose. We would have found it much easier to agree on a wages policy in the 1950s. That, however, is exactly why we did not need one then. Because of our uncertain purpose and our faltering confidence in the overriding value of the society we are evolving through our economic efforts, the disciplines imposed by any incomes policy will often be felt as an imposition. And the angry reaction of one group, tearing through the limits, will stimulate others to do the same. High wage claims in one sector prompt similar claims in others. Taxpayers' revolts increase the bitterness of the poor. Inflation is the visible sign of our disarray and is itself an object of anxiety. It compounds our self-doubt.

To sum up the argument, the modern identity and the accompanying moral visions give the background to both the affirmative and critical stances to our society. They show them to be closely related. But they also help us understand the balance between the two. In fact, the affirmative view does not just praise endless accumulation. It must also be seen as an affirmation of efficacy, of productive power, which in turn is a sign of autonomy and of our domination over things. Thus, the affirmative view is vulnerable to whatever presses on us an understanding of the extent to which we are not in fact autonomous, are not dominating, but are enslaved to things. The word "fetish" is redolent of this. It connects with the earlier rejection of idolatry and the modern's sense of superiority over the primitive, of having won freedom from an obsession in things, from an immersion in them, and from a shaping of one's life on their model.

Now in fact we live in a society whose practices embody a certain notion of identity and the human good. This notion must be ours or we cannot give it our allegiance; we are alienated from it. At the same time, we rely to a great extent on these practices to maintain our sense of identity. If these practices, which supposedly embody the modern identity, can be shown to lead in fact to a failure to achieve it, as noted in the paragraph above, then our allegiance to them is shaken. Perhaps our faith in the conception of the modern identity is shaken as well. We turn to other models.

In the balance between affirmative and negative stances to our society, the affirmative relies largely on the first version of life according to nature, as this has become embedded in the political and economic, largely market-atomistic practices of our society. If we become convinced that we are dominated by mindless forces or enslaved to commodities which we fetishize, then we will withdraw allegiance form these practices and obviously from the first version, or at least from this way of expressing the first version institutionally.

PARTICIPATION AND RIGHTS

Does all this mean that the advanced, industrial-technological, capitalist, liberal society is on a course to self-destruction? Is some version of the hypertrophy story right after all? Something like this might do as a first approximation. But if the above analysis is at all valid, this could turn out to be a dangerous oversimplification. The modern identity of the citizen producer who is a free and equal bearer of rights does not simply destroy itself when it is pushed beyond a certain point. A more accurate way of putting it would be to say that some sides of this identity threaten through hypertrophy to frustrate or undermine others, and hence endanger the whole. Part of the foregoing could be sketchily summarized by saying that our pursuit of efficacy as producers has come to threaten our efficacy as citizens. Another part could be explained by saying that freedom as mobility has begun to destroy the very conditions, in family and citizen community, of the identity of freedom.

But perhaps this catches the main point of the "too-much" view. Of course, the modern identity is complex and many-sided. Its nemesis is that, pushed to a certain point, some of its features must destroy the others. It cannot but self-destruct. But here again, reality is more complex. No one can deny that the modern identity is open to certain kinds of destructive, one-sided hypertrophy. That is to say, a civilization animated by this identity will always experience these temptations. For instance, it will always be tempting for us to go for a one-sided understanding of freedom as residing just in the experience of breaking away, of being on our own, a kind of social and historical atomism. "J'ai eu raison dans tous mes dédains: puisque je m'évade," as Rimbaud expresses it.[13] But to think of this as the drive of the modern identity, which thus has to be tempered in order to avoid self-destruction, is to fail to understand what has been going on over the last centuries – or so I have been arguing. It fails to see that the aspirations to family life, and also to citizen participation, are just as much part of the modern identity, that they grow from the same roots as and are inextricably connected with the drive to modern freedom. What we need in order to overcome the one-sidedness of atomistic freedom lies not in our past but in other facets of the modern identity itself.

This also puts in question that sense of the quasi-inevitability of breakdown which the "too much" story tends to breed, at least the sense that our only hope lies in slowing or moderating the movement to freedom, equality, control, and so on. This is based on a misapprehension. The forms of modernity are multiple. There is more than one way of realizing the constellation of aspirations which make up the modern identity. There is even more than one successful way, as well as countless self-destructive ones, but the latter are not to be considered fuller realizations of modernity than the former.

Seen in this way, the principal challenge to contemporary Western liberal societies like our own seems to concern their nature as citizen republics. More broadly, we might say that the "community" dimensions of modern life, both family and state, are under threat in face of "atomist" perspectives. In the remainder of this chapter, I concentrate on the political dimension.

What emerges from the foregoing is that the contemporary development of the society of growth-concentration-mobility threatens citizen self-rule. Concentration and mobility increase the burden of government. At the same time, the felt need for coordination and more and more massive resources tends to concentrate the functions of government at the centre. As a consequence, the functions of government tend to be both more bureaucratically rigid and more distant from the citizenry. Parallel to this development and aggravating it are the mobility and the decline of local communities, which undermine citizen identification and strengthen atomistic self-understanding. The result is a paradoxical and very threatening process in which the burdens of the public sector increase while the willingness of citizens to assume them steadily decreases. A sense of citizen impotence feeds the atomistic safeguarding of mobility, which in turn aggravates the impotence.

This is the truth behind the "ungovernability" or overload theory described in the first section, as well as behind the sense of threat in ever-increasing atomization and continuous unchecked growth. Contemplating it can easily lead to a fatalistic sense of the inevitability of breakdown, because concentration, growth, and mobility seem so hard to stop. For instance, the demands of modern economic management appear to point irrevocably in this direction. As Huntington puts it, "An increasingly sophisticated economy and active involvement in world affairs seem likely to create stronger needs for hierarchy, bureaucracy, centralization of power, expertise, big government specifically, and big organisations generally."[14] Although he is describing the American case here, it is hard to believe that we won't experience similar pressures in Canada.

But our degrees of freedom may not be so reduced. Not only may it be possible to moderate the trends to growth and concentration, but there may be more than one way of reacting to them even where they are unstoppable, as we shall see. Of course, this is not to deny that the development I have been describing is potentially fatal for a modern society. Logically, one could imagine a stable condition in which citizens settled down to accept a semi-permanent condition of bureaucratic tutelage, tempered by the residual power available every few years to "throw the rascals out." Of course, in a highly bureaucratized government, changing the top political team does not alter things very much, but at least it offers a sort of catharsis to the public. This condition would approach that described in the Schumpeterian élite theories of democracy. What would be sacrificed definitively would be the aspiration to some kind of participatory self-rule. Some people think that the United States, with its startlingly low level of voter participation, is settling into this pattern.

In fact, however, this condition cannot be stable. It is too obviously a truncated way of life relative to the full demands of the modern identity. Any form of tutelage must be unacceptable in the end. A Western society that proceeds too far down this road incurs the risk of a "legitimation crisis." The instructive comparison here is with Soviet society, which for a variety of reasons was kept apart from the mainstream development of Western civil society. All the signs are that bureaucratic tutelage was considered a normal form of rule in the USSR. The contrast is striking if one moves over the border into Poland, a society which participated in early modern times in the Western republican tradition. Here the marriage of national identity with forms of self-rule is a natural one, as the Solidarity movement strikingly illustrated. In any case, in Western society a condition of tutelage is unacceptable because it conflicts with the dignity of a free agent as this is understood in the modern identity. It gives no place to citizen efficacy. So we can understand the strength of the reactions to bureaucratic distance and rigidity in the West.

One of the most important reactions has been the politics of the New Right,[15] which has come to power in both Britain and the United States and is gaining ground elsewhere. This seeks in a sense to reduce the overload on government by transferring a number of economic and even social matters back to the supposedly self-regulating mechanisms of the market. This is meant not only to allow government to work effectively again, thus restoring citizen efficacy, but also to restore to everyone a greater sense of personal efficacy in those matters, which are thus reprivatized.

Private enterprise will supposedly give us back a sense of individual achievement.

I indicated above why I believe that this kind of politics is largely based on an illusion. The overload on government, as well as the increasing alienation from it, comes from the way of life generated by growth, concentration, and mobility – trends which the politics of free enterprise can only accelerate. In spite of all the aggressive rhetoric, no government of the New Right will really be able to undo the welfare state, because it will be in effect increasing the needs that "welfare" measures are designed to meet. Bigger cities, less controlled suburban sprawl, a short-sighted reduction in anti-pollution measures, the erosion of local communities, all these will increase the long-term costs that will inevitably devolve on the public sector.

Less powerful but more coherent is the politics of the ecological left. This involves coming to grips with the trends to growth, concentration, and mobility in two related ways. The first consists in our taking a more selective attitude towards growth; the second, the attempt to decentralize power and decisions. Like the politics of the New Right, the aim is to decrease the overload on centralized, bureaucratized governments. Unlike it, the beneficiaries of the transfer are not individuals in a regime of free enterprise, but are smaller, more accessible public authorities. The aim is to restore citizen efficacy both by reducing the weight of distant, insensitive power and by making the link between public function and citizen input more palpable, as it can be in smaller or more tightly knit political communities. Of course, this kind of politics presupposes that such smaller communities already exist, that they already constitute poles of identification for citizens. Just having a good plan on paper to hand over decisions to hitherto subordinate authorities will accomplish little if these do not correspond to living communities. The politics of the ecological left may not be practicable everywhere.

Both the solutions just described, right and left, involve combatting bureaucratization, and the second comes to grips with the interlocking trends to growth, concentration, and mobility. But other responses are available to the crisis of overload and alienation, which involve not fighting them but living with them. Once again, the contemporary American experience may offer a model.

A striking feature of American political culture compared to ours is its litigiousness. Americans tend to go to the courts to get their rights far more than we and most other Western societies do. They not only do this in suits for private damages – think of the virtual epidemic of malpractice suits that have had an important impact on the practice and economics of medicine in the United States – they also settle important issues of public policy in court. The most spectacular case in recent years was the celebrated decision in *Brown v. the Board of Education* (1954), which outlawed racially segregated schooling.

One can argue that the emphasis on the courts as instruments of political change has increased in the United States over recent decades. This can perhaps be related to the increasing centralization and bureaucratization of American political life, which has been proceeding for at least the last half-century, and in some respects longer.[16] It is not just that the courts as an instrument of change provide an alternative to the legislative process – and thus the more unwieldy the legislative process is, the more people will have recourse to the courts. Something more subtle is at work that has to do with understandings of dignity. This is that the sense of the dignity of the free agent has been identified more with the bearer of rights than with the citizen participator. There are alternative models of society here which are worth bringing out clearly in ideal types, even at the risk of some oversimplification.

In one model, the dignity of the free individual resides in the fact that he has rights that he can make efficacious if necessary even against the process of collective decision making of the society, against the majority will, or the prevailing consensus. The rights he enjoys can be seen as "trumps," in Ronald Dworkin's memorable image;[17] that is, by appeal to them, he can override what normally is decisive – the duly determined outcome of majority will through the legislative process. In the other model, his freedom and efficacy reside in his ability to participate in the process of majority decision making, in having a recognized voice in establishing the "general will." Obviously, a lot more needs to be said to make this distinction clear. In what follows, I refer for convenience simply to the "rights" model and the "participatory" model, respectively. These names could give rise to misunderstandings, which I shall try to head off by some initial explanations.

The first point to stress is that the participatory society does not exclude the entrenching and security of rights. All modern Western societies are founded in some degree on the recognition of rights, and these are open to some degree to judicial defence and retrieval. This was true of Canada before the Constitution Act of 1982 and even before the Bill of Rights of 1960. Legislation and executive action infringing basic rights was upset in the Supreme Court in the Roncarelli case, for instance. It could even be plausibly argued that some recognition of a framework of rights is an essential part of the liberal democratic package in contemporary Western societies. There have to be acknowledged rights to vote, to assemble, to organize parties, and so on. Where these are being denied, they have to be recoverable in the courts, as, for example, the voting rights of Southern blacks in the United States. Moreover, the rights element in our political cultures has been greatly strengthened in recent decades, thanks to an international movement, reflected in the 1946 United Nations Universal Declaration of Human Rights, the constitutions of the ex-colonial states, the increasing saliency of rights tribunals, and the like.

Virtually every polity today claims to be a rights society, and all liberal democratic ones effectively are. But this uniformity leaves room for a number of important issues. One concerns the objects of rights claims. Should they be confined to the centuries-old schedule of negative service rights, whereby individuals are protected in their life, freedoms, inviolability, and the like? Or should we try to entrench other goods – equality, the social promotion of disadvantaged groups, economic security, and the like? The postwar climate has seen a definite move towards extension. Some have welcomed this as a valid expansion of the traditional Western culture of rights. Others have seen a dangerous "inflation," a dangerous distortion of the concept into domains where it is unfitted, which threatens to dislocate the political process.[18]

The distinction I want to draw is closely related to, without collapsing into, this latter issue. It is naturally a feature of what I call rights model societies that they tend to try to attain certain ends – such as the social promotion of disadvantaged groups, or the ensuring of equality – by court action based on rights claims, rather than through mobilizing a majority for legislative action. In the United States, for instance, courts impose electoral redistribution schemes on state governments in the name of equality of citizens and impose detailed plans of affirmative action on hiring institutions in the name of racial and sexual equality. Such decisions in many other countries would have to be made by legislatures.

I am trying to look through these differences about the scope and content of judicially recoverable rights to the underlying understandings of what the citizen's dignity consists in. What I call a rights model society is very likely one where broad social goals are pursued through the courts. But the crucial feature I want to designate is a more elusive one, touching the self-under-standing of members' political identity: What are the capacities that mainly define the dignity of a free individual? In this kind of society it resides crucially in the ability to secure one's rights, even against the political will of the majority.

It should be obvious therefore that a participatory society in this sense is not one in which rights pleas have no place (there are no such societies in the modern democratic world). Nor is it even defined as one in which these pleas are given relatively narrow scope, although it is overwhelmingly likely that it will tend in this direction. This is because what defines this model is that the sense of citizen dignity is based on having a voice in deciding the common laws by which members live. This naturally presupposes that the institutions and practices by which the whole corpus of common laws are established, as well as this corpus itself, enjoy a profound respect in the society, so that our identity is defined in relation to them and dignity is conferred by taking part in them. Special importance attaches to the fact that we as a whole, or community, decide about ourselves as a whole community.[19]

Thus, the participatory model clearly presupposes a strong sense of community identity. I cannot identify my efficacy with my participation in common decisions unless our common lot, the fate of the community, matters a lot to me. By contrast, the first, or rights, model goes very well with a more atomist consciousness, where I understand my dignity as that of an individual bearer of rights. Indeed – and here the tension surfaces between the two – I cannot be too willing to trump the collective decision in the name of individual rights if I have not already moved some dis-tance from the community that makes these decisions. The culture of rights pushed to a certain point, the habit of circumventing majority decision through court judgments, both presupposes and further entrenches taking a distance from community decision making.[20]

This may cast some light on the growth in political litigation in recent decades in America. Of course, the habit of litigation, and the elements of atomist consciousness which go along with it, are deeply rooted in American history. But it may be that the recent increase in reliance on the courts is both a product and then also, once again, a cause of the growing bureaucratic distance of American politics and the consequent citizen alienation which the declining voting figures seem to reflect.[21]

By contrast, Canada has been more identified with the participatory model. By this I do not mean to imply that Canada has an advanced or model democracy or has something to teach the world in republican virtue. I mean only that over the postwar decades, as the sense of citizen dignity has developed in all modern societies, it has tended in Canada to take the participatory rather than the rights forms. This is not to say that it has developed as much as it might or as much as it ought. It can be argued that there is still too much deference in Canadian politics. Indeed, it has been argued that crucial elements of the participatory model in our country – for instance, our legislative institutions and the widespread respect for established law – have their origins in the hierarchical and deferential past of British North America, in contrast to the republic to the south. That is as may be. This brief overview does not argue the interesting question of origins or take a stand on the Hartz-Horowitz thesis about the Tory origins of English Canada.[22]

Whether the origins are in such long-standing traditions of political culture or in the relative weakness and vulnerability of Canadian regional societies, the undoubted consequence has been a greater respect for government and a more welcome acceptance of government initiative and action than there is south of the border – from the Canadian Pacific Railway in the nineteenth century through to Medicare and the National Energy Policy. Whatever the causes, the Canadian frontier was policed by the Mounties[23] rather than by the free-lance figures dramatized in our day by John Wayne or Ronald Reagan (not only, alas, in his earlier profession). All this cannot be without effect on our sense of citizen dignity and has turned it without doubt towards the participatory model. Whether this has also restrained or even crippled it is another question, which I will not go into here, except to say that claims to this effect seem to me at best vastly exaggerated. The Canadians of today are not an excessively deferential people.

Does the fact that we have taken on for the first time an entrenched bill of rights and hence have immensely increased the scope of judicial decision (potentially at least) mean that we are deserting this tradition for something closer to the American model? Only time will tell, but I doubt it. Or rather, an entrenched bill by itself could not lead to the massive transfer of our understanding of the dignity of free agency from the participatory to the rights mode, which would align us with current American practice.

A politics of rights can combine easily with another feature that has been in evidence in the United States and elsewhere in recent years – the growth of single-issue politics. What both these trends have in common is that they are less concerned with the overall set of decisions about the common affairs of society, which have to be arrived at and made minimally consistent, than they are about the outcome of the issue in question. Both combine all too easily with a disinterest in, even contempt for, the institutions and practices through which these decisions are hammered out and rendered consistent – for example, parties and parliaments. Participatory politics, on the other hand, presupposes that these institutions and practices are valued and cherished as the locus of the citizen life. In contrast to this, the slogan for much contemporary politics in America could be the motto of that dynasty which the colonies had to rebel against to found their republic: "Dieu et mon droit."

Nevertheless, the developments I described above may suggest that a transfer of this kind is inevitable – either because it will ineluctably come to pass or because it is our best hope. If modern society is heading for irreversible bureaucratization and centralization, and if this is inescapably accompanied by an increasing atomization, then maybe the best way to rescue and give expression to the dignity of free agents is by a greater and greater emphasis on the defence of rights through court action. Seen in this perspective, the Constitution of 1982 comes at exactly the right moment to provide the legal framework for this new departure. It will provide something that has been missing in Canadian history hitherto and will make up for what must be seen as our incredible backwardness in exploiting the penalties of redress through the courts.[24]

Before we can say whether this kind of transfer is either inevitable or advisable, what we need to do is understand something more about the bases of the participatory model in Canadian society. The condition for a successful participatory model is a strong identification with the fate of the community. In the long history of analysis and discussion of the bases of republican self-rule in our civilization, from Greek times through the Romans to those moderns who took up this tradition, this sense of community identification has been variously described – sometimes as "patriotism," sometimes as "virtue" (Montesquieu's word), sometimes in terms of its opposite, "corruption" (Machiavelli's description). It is the elusive factor which is thought to make a participatory regime viable while its absence beyond a certain point makes despotism inevitable. The reasoning behind this belief in its many forms is that only such a strong identification with the society could move citizens to assume willingly the heavier burdens of a free regime,[25] while the failure of this identification would require that even the lesser burdens of a despotism be imposed by force.

This identification can perhaps be described in this way: it exists where the common form of life is seen as a supremely important good, so that its continuance and flourishing matters to the citizens for its own sake and not just instrumentally to their several individual goods or as the sum total of these individual goods. The common life has a status of this kind when it is a crucial element in the members' identity, in the modern, Eriksonian sense of the term; hence my use of "identification."

But it is useful to separate analytically two elements in this common identity. First, the common life must be one partly defined in terms of the political formula of participation itself. The subjects of a divinely appointed despot may identify as such and may be moved to feats of self-sacrificial dedication on the battlefield, but this has nothing to do with the maintenance of a republican regime. That is why, in the literature and rhetoric of republican regimes, the common life which is the focus of identity is so often described as "the laws."[26] There is an inner connection between the common focus and the dignity that accompanies citizenship: the institutions and practices of equal participation are the common condition of the dignity of each, while this dignity in turn is defined in terms of contribution to the health and survival of these laws. The second analytically separable aspect of a common identity is that these laws must in fact serve to unite a specific community. It is not sufficient, in other words, that one simply live in a society where participatory institutions and practices prevail, even if one values them. Unless there is a common sense of a determinate community whose members sense a bond between them from this common allegiance, an identification with the common good cannot arise.

Of course, in ancient poleis and republics, these two conditions went naturally together. It seems artificial to separate them. In modern liberal society, however, they can come apart. Contemporary societies can be strongly bonded by a sense of common life where this is not defined in terms of the institutions of liberal participation or sometimes not even in terms of any political institutions. Most spectacularly, they can be bound together by a national or ethnic identification. On the other hand, people can live together under a common liberal democratic regime, and prize this, without feeling a strong bond of community with the other members as members, but perhaps having a stronger identification with some subset of its citizens or perhaps with some supranational community. Living in Canada, of course, makes one acutely aware of the various ways in which institutional and community allegiance can be out of phase with each other.

Rather schematically, one can say that the two important poles of common identification in the Western liberal world are participatory institutions on one hand and ethnic or national appartenance on the other, where national identity is frequently defined in terms of language – at least in European-derived cultures. How these two relate in any given society matters a great deal to the form, the health, and ultimately the survival of democratic regimes.

In some sense, the happiest relationship is that found in Britain and the Netherlands, where participatory institutions are thought to be an integral part of the national culture. A kind of happy chauvinism can have free reign here, where representative government can be seen as a national invention imitated in more or less botched form by lesser breeds of foreigners. At the other extreme are countries such as prewar Spain and Italy, where powerful political forces espoused a definition of the national culture which vigorously excluded democratic institutions. France, throughout the postrevolutionary period up to the aftermath of World War II, suffered from a lack of national consensus on the basic political formula. For important strands of opposition during the Third Republic, the true French national identity demanded the overthrow of republican institutions. Another kind of historic lack of fit has been evident in the Federal Republic of Germany in recent years. There has been a strong attachment to democratic institutions, but this sits so uneasily athwart significant strands of modern German history that the attachment to democracy has gone along with a deliberate distancing from national sentiment and affirmation (which has at once excited the wonder of foreigners and been a cause of continuing anxiety lest it suddenly give way to the opposite extreme). Something like this division with a national culture over the identification with democratic institutions exists in the past of French Canada as well. As with the European societies of Latin culture, which strongly influenced us, this rejection of democracy was deeply discredited by the experience of fascism and World War II; and the welding of liberal democracy and national identification is as complete in Quebec today as in any other Western society.

In contrast to Latin cultures, where national identity and liberal representative institutions had to be brought to fusion (in some cases, through struggle and civil war), and in contrast to the British case, where these institutions are seen as a feature of the national identity, the United States seems to offer the example of a nation that owes its identity to the common acceptance of a political formula. This produces something analogous to the British case – a strong sense of national identity inextricably defined in terms of certain political institutions, known roughly as "the American way of life." But the fact that the political formula has been the original pole of allegiance, rather than the institutions, has made a big difference. It has given American liberalism that militant quality which has produced the best and the worst in U.S. history – both the ability to integrate millions of new citizens from other, non-Anglo-Saxon cultures and to undertake great reforms like those achieved by the civil rights movements in our time, and also the propensity to prosecute deviants for "un-American activities." This militancy has had important effects on American foreign policy as well, very notably but not exclusively in the rhetoric of moral universal which informs it. No one can deny that this difference in rhetorical self-perception has had important consequences for world history, all the way from Woodrow Wilson's Fourteen Points to Reagan's ravings about the "evil empire."

The bipolarity of focus – institutional and national – exists everywhere in the modern advanced world where any form of common life is recognized as a pole of political identity. This duality seems to be ineradicable; or if one pole were to go, it would be the institutional. Perhaps certain Latin American societies – for instance, Argentina – offer examples of unipolarity, where the only possible focus of common identity is national fervour, mobilized at such moments as the World Cup or the Malvinas War. But these are not happy models, and they seem for the moment fortunately distant from us.[27]

I hope that the above discussion has set the terms in which we can come to grips with the historic conditions for the participatory model in Canada. The obvious dilemma it poses for us is that the two poles of identity cannot now or, perhaps, ever simply be superimposed. It is not even that we have a national identity that does not line up with our institutional allegiances, as in earlier Latin cultures. Within a general consensus about democratic liberal institutions, we do not have and cannot develop a single national identity.

The biggest single reason for this is the existence of Quebec. Quebec has a strong sense of national identity, but of a kind that the majority of English-speaking North Americans find unfamiliar – connected to a national language, and moreover one that is under threat. Because of this threat, the preservation and health of this language will always be one of the major national goals of French-speaking Canadians. This involves the continual development of the language as a medium of expression for the full gamut of activities which define modern civilization – politics, technology, art, economic management, communications media, and so on.[28]

In the rest of Canada, on the other hand, language cannot be understood in these terms and it seems strange that it should be a central object of policy as it inevitably is for Quebeckers. Since English is virtually the world hegemonic language today, it is difficult for those who speak it even to understand what it could be like to live under linguistic threat. Rather than seeing language as the indispensable basis of self-expression and self-realization, anglophone North Americans tend to see it as an unproblematic medium of communication. This attitude is strengthened by the fact that both English Canada and the United States are immigrant societies which have received and integrated into the dominant culture countless immigrants from a host of different cultures and languages of origin. The experience of being an assimilating culture tends to change the status of the dominant language. By the very nature of things, it is not everyone's original home language or language of cultural memory, prayer, or continuing ethnic identity. It is these things for many people, of course, but the only status it has for everyone is that of the publicly established medium of communication. The idea that any language could be recognized as the publicly supported medium of self-expression seems in this context bizarre, if not unjust.

To make the misunderstanding complete, until recently French Canada has not had the experience of assimilating masses of immigrants, so the distinction between ethnic and public language has yet to be forced into consciousness in Quebec. Thus, we have the makings of the kind of cross-purposes and deeply felt mutual misunderstanding which recent events in Manitoba once more brought to the fore. What is seen by one group as the indispensable minimum of public recognition that is essential to their survival as a linguistic community is seen by others as the imposition of one community's language on all the rest. In fact, the status demanded for the French language cannot fit into the categories of an immigrant culture as this is understood in North America, because it clearly cannot be the common medium and because francophones are not content to have it remain merely a language of ethnic identity. That French Canadians should fight so strongly against the kind of marginalization of language that the latter status entails seems unwarranted and unjust according to the ground rules of an immigrant society as hitherto understood.

Up to this day there has never been a commonly understood formula of national identity in Canada. Various political arrangements have been negotiated, and something like common understanding of what these involve has existed among those political elites who negotiated them, but no common formula has ever been accepted across Canada by the population at large. In French Canada, the traditional interpretation of the Confederation has been as a pact between "two nations." In this understanding, Canada is a binational state and allegiance to the whole is via allegiance to the part – one adheres to the larger entity because this is the political home which the nation has chosen for itself.[29] The rest of Canada is seen in this view as making up another "nation," which is similarly the primary focus of allegiance for its members and the channel through which they belong to the larger whole. But this has never been the way the rest of Canada sees the country. Certain deeply rooted historical communities, perhaps only Newfoundland today, may see themselves as Canadians only via the adherence of their community to the federal union, but by and large non-French Canadians have a sense of belonging to Canada that is on the same level if not more fundamental than their sense of belonging to a regional or ethnic society. "Unhyphenated" Canadianism is an allegiance beyond and unconditioned by membership in any partial community. Anything less than this seems a formula for breakup in an immigrant society.

This is our great historical misunderstanding, which has shaped Canadian politics for the last century. Each side would require the other to be something it is not in order to fit the formula within which it can itself be comfortable. Ideally, for French Canadians, "English" Canada should be a nation, in the sense of a constituent entity of a binational state. For the rest of Canada, the problem would be solved if only French Canadians would see their French identity as another ethnic identity, enriching but not undercutting an unconditional Canadian allegiance. This way of putting it is oversimplified and understates the progress that has been made on both sides in recent decades towards understanding the other's viewpoint; but a lot yet remains of our historical misunderstanding, and the day when we come to a common definition of the Canadian union which is complex enough to encompass these two quite different perspectives is still a long way off.

In addition to this basic Canadian misunderstanding, the sense of national identity in non-French Canada is complex and in some ways not ultimately defined. It is made up of a number of strands which, while they may not be in conflict, have not yet come together into a stable synthesis. One strand is the traditional allegiance which many people in English Canada feel to their British roots. This is of special relevance to our theme here, because this sense of identity focuses very strongly on the political institutions and practices which are central to the British tradition – for instance, parliamentary government and, of course, the monarchy. Naturally, this is an allegiance which many "ethnic" Canadians do not feel or feel less strongly. Among people of non-British origin, one often finds another powerful strand of Canadian allegiance. This is a sense of Canada's exceptional status as a haven where a certain freedom, dignity, and economic opportunity is at least in principle open to everyone, in strong contrast to the conditions prevailing in other parts of the world, and especially in some of the countries of origin of these new Canadians themselves. The spirit of this sense of Canada is captured in an anecdote from David Lewis. He recalled his astonishment, soon after his arrival, at seeing a policeman guiding schoolchildren safely across the street. The idea that uniformed representatives of authority could be anything other than a menace was something radically new to this adolescent from the Pale of Settlement who had lived through the last years of tsardom and the early years of the revolution and civil war. That policemen could actually do something benign seemed almost too much to accept, and it took some persuasion from older relatives before David Lewis did so.[30]

This sense of identity is especially important for this discussion, because it centres on political institutions and practices of a liberal society, based on the rule of law and the defence of rights and self-rule. In this respect it is analogous to the parallel feelings experienced by generations of immigrants in the United States. But whereas in the United States a perfect fit prevails between this immigrant sentiment and the dominant conception of the national identity (which was also defined in terms of a political formula), in Canada there is a potential division between the traditional "British" and "immigrant" definitions of the Canadian allegiance. Insofar as the British allegiance is itself defined partly by liberal political institutions, a congruence is possible.[31] But should there ever be a move to "rationalize" our political institutions to bring them more in line with foreign models, or to purge the British element on the grounds that this only has meaning for part of our population, then these two strands will come apart. It can be argued that the Trudeau government was not entirely sensitive to this danger and made a number of tentative moves in this direction which threatened to embroil us in another controversy over national identity. For the moment, however, this potential source of misunderstanding is quiescent.

Another not fully resolved question in "English" Canada is that of regionalism. Here, too, there are conflicting mutual perspectives. It would be tidy if the different regions shared the same views about the relative importance of regionalism, but they do not. By and large, Ontarians see themselves not as constituting a "region" – which is how they are seen from the outside – but as being in the centre of Canada. Ontario seems to be the only province in which the regional government is seen as much less significant than the federal government. If the figures for voter participation are any index, all other regions show at least as strong and sometimes a stronger identification with provincial governments than with the federal.[32] From the Ontario perspective, provincial governments sometimes appear just as the large-scale municipalities that Henri Bourassa feared they would be reduced to, but this view does not seem to be widely shared in the rest of the country.

In fact, Canada is a country of strong regional identities. From the outside, even Ontario stands out as a distinct identity, with the particular feature that it does not adequately appreciate from the inside how different it is from the rest. Of course, distinct regional identities are a feature of many societies, particularly in this hemisphere. They are the basis of the federal political solution which so many have adopted, not only in the United States but also in Mexico and Brazil. In other federal societies, however, there has been a great concentration of power over the years in the hands of the central government in response to the needs for development and in some cases for equalization between regions. Regional governments have become subordinate. In Canada, although the federal government has taken large-scale initiatives in development and although regional equalization has become a major theme of Canadian politics, this kind of centralization has always been countered by affirmations of provincial power. The balance has tilted, now towards the centre, now towards the periphery, instead of moving steadily towards concentration.[33]

One major reason for this, of course, has been the determination of French Canada, as incarnate in Quebec, to resist centralization at all costs. But important features of "English" Canada also have contributed to the outcome. In fact, the drive to centralization requires some underlying agreement on national identity, at least some dominant formula, and this has been missing even in "English" Canada. The dominant formula could be defined either institutionally, as in the United States, or in terms of a clearly dominant historical-linguistic identification to which new arrivals are to be unquestionably assimilated, as in Mexico and Brazil. But Canada could opt for neither of these. Our origins as British North America preclude the militant identification with a paradigm political definition, and our nature as an immigrant society, as well as the existence of French Canada, preclude making all the new arrivals "British."

In consequence, although there have been times when central power significantly advanced, the political conditions in the form of a determinate common will – which might have made this irreversible – have always been missing. Canadian provincial governments have by and large kept control of their jurisdictions, including such vital ones as natural resource development. Their budgets are a significant proportion of public-sector activity in Canada.[34] They have real political clout. Nationally sponsored policies in a host of areas have to proceed much more by negotiation between the levels, rather than just through federally sponsored and financed initiatives, than they do in other federal systems in this hemisphere.

This peculiar history lies behind the continuing power of regional identification in Canada. But this is also the locus of another unresolved issue in our national identity, because many

Canadians experience this strength of the regions as a kind of disunity or disarray. Having a central government that has to proceed so much by negotiation in tackling common problems seems to them synonymous with having a weak central government. The value of having a federal government at all seems to them bound up with having a senior government that can tackle national issues, just as the federal government does in other federations, particularly the United States.[35]

It is true that Canadians in general have a rather bewildering combination of political attitudes. We tend to expect a great deal from our federal union in development and equalization policy, while regional identification remains politically significant in a way that is unparalleled in similar federations. There are times when governing Canada seems as intractable a problem as squaring the circle. This can be represented as an ambivalence that ought to be resolved, rather than as a duality of focus that is natural to a federal system. It might appear that in this case the logical resolution we should be working towards is the generation of some such common political will as has enabled other federations to concentrate power. But at this point we connect up again with the original concern underlying this discussion of national identity, namely, the historical conditions of the participatory model in Canada. How does the prospect of centralization look from this point of view?

The condition of successful participatory politics is a strong identification with the community. This condition in turn can be analytically separated into an identification with participatory forms of politics as central to the community's definition and a strong sense of a particular community as bound together in these forms. The first condition is fortunately present in Canada. Of the three perspectives I described on national identity, two – the "British" and the "immigrant" – are partly defined in terms of liberal politics, and the third – that of French Canada – has moved historically to an identification with this kind of politics. It is the other analytically separable condition which makes the problem in Canada. If we look at both the unresolved issues in our national identity and the strands which define these issues, it appears evident that the health of the participatory model in Canada is bound up with continuing regional decentralization. To put the same point negatively, participatory politics would be endangered by a centralizing move.

This seems so on two levels. First, greater centralization of power could only bring with it greater identification with the centre if we resolve the issues still outstanding in our common understanding of the national identity. It seems utopian, to put it mildly, to hope that this might happen in the near or even middle future. Even if we imagine the issue about regionalism to be resolved by hypothesis, as the precondition for centralization, we are still nowhere near resolving the latent tension between the "British" and "immigrant" identities. As for the misunderstanding between French and English Canada, it is hard to imagine how this could ever by resolved around a formula that would permit greater centralization. This brings us to the second level. Even if we are very optimistic about the evolution of mutual understanding in this country, it is difficult to imagine viable common resolutions that would not incorporate a healthy dose of decentralized politics. Is there really a viable solution to the regionalism issue in Canada that would just set us on something like the American road, overriding the strong regional political identities of the Maritime provinces or the West? This seems to me wildly out of phase with the way political life has developed in this country. As for a scenario in which Quebec would be happy within a more centralized Canada, this appears utterly beyond the reach of the wildest imaginings.

The fate of the participatory model in Canada, of the continued health of our practices of self-rule, depends on our continuing resistance to centralization – both because we need many more decades in which to work out the outstanding issues in our common understanding as a political entity and because any such successful resolution itself is bound to involve decentralized power. A basic fact about Canada, which we often have trouble accepting, is that we are still far from achieving a universally agreed definition of our country as a political community, in the rich sense which Donald Smiley, drawing on Aristotle, gives this phrase.[36] Moves towards centralization all too often just seem to assume this lack. In doing so, they not only court failure but risk aborting the long and difficult process through which we may come to this common identity.

These considerations, drawn from our particular case, tell in the same direction as the more general considerations which emerged from the earlier discussion. If our response to the increase of overload and alienation is not to be that of abandoning participatory politics and compensating for this with more effective methods of judicial redress and single-issue campaigning – if our aim is to defend participation – then the only viable policy seems to include some devolution of power, following what I described above as the politics of the ecological left. If our aim is to combat rather than adjust to the trends to growth, concentration, and mobility, and the attendant bureaucratic opacity and rigidity of representative democracy, then some measures of decentralization are indispensable, with the consequent strengthening of more localized, smaller-scale units of self-rule.[37]

These can, of course, take many forms. Decentralized self-rule need not be regional. It can include devolving responsibility for self-management onto employees, giving recipients and beneficiaries a say in the operation of public programs, giving more responsibilities back to school boards, and a host of other measures. But, certainly, keeping power at the regional level in a federation like ours is one very effective form of decentralization, ensuring that important issues are within the scope of communities that not only are smaller and less unwieldy but that frequently have a higher degree of community identification than the nation from coast to coast.

Of course, this direction is not without its dangers and difficulties. Canada will face immense problems in the stiffening economic competition of the years ahead. Avoiding deindustrialization, maintaining and increasing our rate of technological innovation, avoiding mutually stultifying internal rivalry such as the fragmentation of the Canadian market through provincial regulations,[38] and finding the resources for the necessary large-scale development projects will all generate a growing need for coordinated activity. This will put progressively greater strain on our resources of political leadership and vision, and on the ability and readiness to generate ever-new consensus. In many ways it would be easier, given the bent of late-twentieth-century technology and economic integration, to be under the aegis of a more centralized, bureaucratic governmental authority, for all its irrationalities and foul-ups, and for all the alienation of citizens from political power that it entails. If our political leadership is not up to it, we may indeed have to settle for something like this as the only alternative to stagnation and economic regression.

HAVE WE A CHOICE?

To evoke this troubling perspective is to bring us back to the central theme of this chapter. After surveying all the pressures to unchecked growth, concentration, and mobility, and weighing the threats and challenges that may drive us to premature centralization, we may be tempted to feel that the future direction of our development as a nation is inexorably fixed – that we cannot but go the road of greater centralization and bureaucracy, with the inevitable consequences of atomism and citizen alienation. But it is this sense of the inevitability of breakdown, or at least of the tendency to breakdown as implicit in the very identity and forms of life which have arisen in the modern era, that I have tried to combat throughout this chapter.

Perhaps it might be useful here to draw the threads together in order to make this point once more. The discussion of the modern identity was meant to show this as more complex and less one-sided than it is usually portrayed. Certainly, the modern understandings of freedom and efficacy tend to breed atomism and to undermine community. But the same emphasis on efficacy has also helped to create contemporary understandings of citizen dignity, and this has sometimes been the basis of renewed community identification and solidarity around institutions of self-rule. Certainly, modern efficacy has tended to breed an exploitative stance towards nature, heedless of the demands of ecological balance. But the post-Romantic sense of kinship with nature comes, if I am right, from the same complex of self-understandings. Undoubtedly, again, the modern conception of self-fulfilment has played havoc with marital stability and the securities of family life. But the same focus on sexual and emotional fulfilment as central to the meaning of life has made us search for new forms and modes of family relationship.

Modern history is not unilinear, not an inexorable progress or decline, or a progress which entails decline. Rather, it is made up of movements and counter-movements in which typically modern dangers have bred typically modern defences. In this domain, the famous line form Hölderlin, often quoted by Heidegger, seems to hold true: *Wo aber Gefahr ist, wächst / Das Rettende auch.*[39] And so, while it is possible to trace a pattern of breakdown, in which the trends to growth, concentration, and mobility reinforce each other virtually without limit, this will almost always be an abstraction from a much more complex reality. Vicious circles are easy to find. There is undoubtedly a pressure to unrestrained production for a higher consumer standard in disregard of ecological and social priorities. This undoubtedly contributes to the higher mobility that undermines traditional local communities and brings about massive concentration of populations. These factors both contribute to bureaucratic distance and hence to citizen alienation and cynicism, which in turn make people even less inclined to be concerned for social priorities and hence even more undivided in their fixation on the consumer standards. But at each point in this spiral decline, counter-forces – the attachment to the land (sometimes a very strong force in Canada), a sense of threatened community, a new style of family life – may be at work. Supposedly inexorable movements are sometimes surprisingly reversed, such as the drift from smaller towns towards larger cities, which seems to have gone the other way in the United States in the last decade. Even the supposed drive to big bureaucratic enterprise in the name of economic efficiency turns out to be not all that ineluctable either, as is shown by the success of a new style of management that relies on smaller, more flexible interdisciplinary teams.

Of course, my point is not to replace Spenglerian gloom by Panglossian optimism. I am not saying that every lurch towards destruction will meet its equal and opposite defence. Rather, my aim is to argue that the outcome can go either way. If I am right, the conclusion is not greater security but greater contingency in modern history. Some societies will fall apart, or at least have to regress to more bureaucratized, authoritarian forms to hold together. But none need be considered as doomed beforehand.

This reflection brings us back to Canada. What are our chances in the late twentieth century? To make a global judgment, one would have to look at the whole range of challenges which tend to interlock in their effects on contemporary society. We would have to gauge how ready or able we are to determine the direction of our economic growth in the name of ecological limits and social priorities. We would have to understand more about the evolution of family life in our country. We would have to examine the bases and nature of our sense(s) of political community. In this chapter, I have been addressing myself exclusively to the last question. Even here, the discussion makes no claim to comprehensiveness. It would be a very ambitious undertaking indeed to assess the health and stability of Canadian society across the board. Intuitively, it sometimes appears that Canada on the whole is a society where people care more for their roots than people do in the United States, and hence where family and local community are under less severe straining. But the future may show this to be a complacent illusion.

We have perhaps no great grounds for complacency in regard to our sense of citizen dignity and identification. But these have developed a particular character in this country, and my argument has been that to fail to respect this is to put us in peril. My case might be summed up in two propositions: (a) that our sense of citizen dignity is closer to what I called the participatory model than the rights model; and (b) that the combination of an unresolved national identity as Canadians and the strength of our historical regional societies makes it virtually mandatory for us to practise a more decentralized style of government than other comparable federations. This, of course, puts tremendous demands on our political leadership and our ability to generate continuing consensus. Should this fail, we may be forced to some more centralized mode.

If, however, we look at Canada's future in the perspective central to this chapter – that is, in terms of the way this country can best face the strains of modernity and the dangers of political breakdown implicit in them – there seems no doubt that the centralizing solution would be an immensely regressive step. Looked at in the light of the full demands of the modern identity, the atrophy of citizen power negates an important dimension of our dignity as free agents and hence poses a potential long-term threat to the legitimacy of a modern society.

True, the American case shows us a model whereby this can be compensated by a political culture that allows very wide scope for the defence of rights. If we go the centralizing route, we will undoubtedly have at the same time to approach this model very closely – a development for which our entrenched bill of rights may have provided the foundation. In a sense, to oversimplify and dramatize, we can see two package solutions emerging out of the mists to the problem of sustaining a viable modern polity in the late twentieth century. One is the route of political centralization, at the cost of some citizen alienation but compensated for by an increasing incorporation of the American model in which dignity finds political expression in the defence of rights. The other is the route of continued decentralization, and a continued attempt to maintain and extend our historical participatory model, at the cost of putting a greater and greater strain on political vision and inventiveness through mechanisms of political coordination.

Perhaps only one of these – or neither – will prove to be viable; perhaps we are already irrevocably embarked on one. These outcomes are hard to foretell. But if we ask which of these solutions is better suited to meet the strains of modernity, there is little doubt in my mind that the decentralizing one has the edge. It is not just that this solution is more in line with our traditional political culture, including the very docility in accepting the law as decided, with which Americans (and sometimes even we ourselves) reproach us. It is also that severe doubts still hang over the entire long-term viability of the rights model as a safeguard for the dignity of the modern free agent. Can it really substitute for the sense of having a say in the common decision? Could the increasing stress on rights as dominant over collective decisions come in the end to undermine the very legitimacy of the democratic order? As these questions are being asked by thoughtful Americans, it would be reckless for us to force ourselves against the grain of history onto a path whose end point is in such doubt.

Notes

1 See his *Capitalism, Socialism and Democracy,* 3d ed. (New York: Harper and Row, 1950); also Robert Dahl, *Preface to Democratic Theory* (Chicago: University of Chicago Press, 1956).
2 See the interesting discussion in Claus Offe, "'Ungovernability': The Renaissance of Conservative Theories of Crisis," reprinted in C. Offe,

Contradictions of the Welfare State (Cambridge, Mass.: MIT Press, 1984). Offe shows how much common ground there is between "overload" theories of the left and the right. An influential formulation of the former perspective was James O'Connor's *Fiscal Crisis of the State* (New York: St Martin's Press, 1973). For a recent discussion of the American scene from the latter perspective, see Samuel Huntington, *American Politics: The Promise of Disharmony* (Cambridge, Mass.: Harvard University Press, 1981).

3 Daniel Bell, *Cultural Contradictions of Capitalism* (New York: Basic, 1976), especially chap. 1.

4 For an interesting contemporary theory aimed at the rescue of the goods implicit in modernity, see J. Habermas, *Theorie des Kommunikativen Handelns* (*Theory of Communicative Action*) (Boston: Beacon Press, 1983). The connection of this kind of theory with reform politics is evident, in this case, in a form that is entirely freed from the illusions of original Marxism about socialism as the fruit of a breakdown of capitalism.

5 See J. Habermas, *Legitimation Crisis* (Boston: Beacon Press, 1975).

6 See L. Stone, *The Family, Sex and Marriage in England 1500–1800* (London: Weidenfeld and Nicolson, 1977).

7 Michel Foucault, *Surveiller et punir* (Paris, 1976); trans. as *Discipline and Punish* (London: Allen Lane, 1977).

8 See J. Rawls, *A Theory of Justice* (Boston: Harvard University Press, 1971); and R. Nozick, *Anarchy, State and Utopia* (Boston: Basic, 1974). Rawls himself is by no means a prisoner of the atomist perspective.

9 See Bell, *Cultural Contradictions of Capitalism*. I think Bell gives too much importance to the signs of a more positive valuation of hedonism in contemporary America; or, better, he puts this valuation in the wrong context. What happened in the 1960s and 1970s was not just a collapse of the old "Protestant ethic" into mere "permissiveness." To see things this way is to look at the whole development from the outside. But this utterly leaves out of account the moral passion and earnestness of this phase of youth culture across the Western world.

10 Fred Somkin, *Unquiet Eagle* (Ithaca: Cornell University Press, 1967).

11 E. Schumacher, *Small Is Beautiful* (New York: Harper and Row, 1973), 30.

12 H. Stretton, *Capitalism, Socialism and the Environment* (Cambridge: Cambridge University Press, 1976), 224.

13 Arthur Rimbaud, *Une Saison en enfer: L'Impossible* (Paris: Gallimard, 1973).

14 Huntington, *American Politics,* 228.

15 I realize that what is often called the "New Right" is a more complex phenomenon than is described here. I have singled out the strand that exalts individual initiative and free enterprise at the expense of government action. But there are sometimes other aspirations, such as revitalization of local government, or volunteer collective action, which overlap with what I describe below as the politics of the ecological left. But this "atomist" strand is worth singling out because a lot of controversial policies of right-leaning governments today turn on it alone.

16 See the interesting argument by Michael Sandel, in his "Procedural Republic and the Unencumbered Self," *Political Theory* 12 (February 1984): 81–96, that the increased emphasis on a definition of liberal democracy in terms of rights follows the centralization of government and the not entirely successful attempts to "nationalize" American politics, i.e., creates a strong sense of political community at the national level (esp. 92–3). For a fuller background to Sandel's argument, see his *Liberalism and the Limits of Justice* (Cambridge: Cambridge University Press, 1982).

17 See Dworkin's "Liberalism," in *Public and Private Morality,* ed. by Stuart Hampshire (Cambridge: Cambridge University Press, 1978).

18 For the "inflation" view, see Tom Pocklington, "Against Inflating Human Rights," in *The Windsor Yearbook of Access to Justice,* vol. 2, 1982, cited in Cynthia Williams, "The Changing Nature of Citizen Rights," in *Constitutionalism, Citizenship and Society in Canada,* vol. 33 of the research studies prepared for the Royal Commission on the Economic Union and Development Prospects for Canada (Toronto: University of Toronto Press, 1985). Williams also gives an interesting discussion of this issue. I have tried to distinguish different notions of rights in my "Les Droits de l'homme," forthcoming in a volume to be published by UNESCO.

19 As Rousseau puts it, the general will is attained only when "tout le peuple statue sur tout le peuple" (*Contrat social,* 2.6).

20 It follows from this that not all the measures associated traditionally with radical demand for "participatory democracy" necessarily strengthen what I call the participatory model. A constitution may call for referenda, recall of legislators, citizens' initiatives, election of

judges, and the like; but it can easily be that the use to which these are put, and even the spirit in which they are adopted, involve scant respect for the general will. Rather, they may be designed and used to ensure the individual's or subgroup's ability to defend itself, even against the majority and the highest legislative institutions. Think of the use of citizen initiative in California, for instance, in the tax revolt of 1978 (the famous Proposition 13). This kind of politics takes over and amends the traditional slogan, *fiat justitia, ruat coelum*. In the case of Proposition 13, the amendment might read, "Let my property taxes decline, though the welfare state collapse." It is hard to imagine anything more antithetical to the spirit of community identification.

21 Thus, voter participation in off-year congressional elections dropped from 55.4 per cent in 1966 to 44.7 per cent in 1974, rising somewhat to 48.5 per cent in 1982. In presidential elections the decline seems to have been steady over the last decades, from 69.3 per cent in 1964 to 59.2 per cent in 1980 (source: current population reports; *Special Studies*, series s23, no. 130, *Population Profile of the United States, 1982*, U.S. Department of Commerce, Bureau of the Census, 23–33). Two separate points seem to arise from these figures: (a) the trend downward over recent decades, and (b) the generally low level compared with other democracies, where voter turnout is often over 70 per cent, and in cases like Saskatchewan provincial elections with turnouts of over 80 per cent. It has been persuasively argued that (b) is largely due to the eccentricity of the U.S. political system, in which voter registration is generally still the citizen's responsibility, whereas just about everywhere else voter's lists are compiled by public authority. There is evidence that this accounts for a big part of the difference with other democracies. Nelson Polsby and Aaron Wildavsky, in their *Presidential Elections: Strategies of American Electoral Policies* (New York: Scribners, 1980), 241, point to the case of Idaho, where registration is carried out on public initiative. Here voter turnout in 1968 was 72.8 per cent, which was comparable to that in Canada and the United Kingdom.

22 See Gad Horowitz, *Canadian Labour in Politics* (Toronto: University of Toronto Press, 1968), chap. 1; and Louis Hartz, *The Liberal Tradition in America* (New York: Harcourt Brace Jovanovich, 1962) and *The Founding of New Societies* (New York: Harcourt Brace Jovanovich, 1969).

23 See S.D. Clark, "The Canadian Community and the American Continental System," in *The Developing Canadian Community* (Toronto: University of Toronto Press, 1968).

24 In spite of the importance of certain crucial court decisions in Canadian history – think of the Roncarelli case in connection with the Padlock Act or the more recent decisions about unilingual Manitoba legislation – Canadians appear to Americans as inexplicably supine and long-suffering when it comes to redress of grievance. Have you tried to explain to an American why, although the violations of Manitoba's bilingual status start in 1890, the first successful challenge only reached the Supreme Court in 1979? From an American perspective it looks as though it took the injured party almost ninety years to take the obvious steps. How does one explain this from a Canadian perspective? I am not quite sure myself. South of the border, there is only one conceivable explanation – we are accustomed to sitting there and taking it without murmur; we lack a lively sense of our own worth and our own rights. Canadians are just backward.

25 Rousseau put it with characteristic force in his *Considérations sur le Gouvernement de Pologne:* "La liberté est un aliment de bon suc, mais de forte digestion; il faut des estomacs sains pour le supporter. Je ris de ces peuples avilis qui ... s'imaginent que, pour être libres, il suffit d'être des mutins. Fière et saine liberté! si ces pauvres gens pouvaient te connaître, s'ils savaient à quel prix on t'acquiert et te conserve; s'ils sentaient combien tes lois sont plus austères que n'est dur le joug des tyrans, leurs faibles âmes, esclaves de passions qu'il faudrait étouffer, te craindraient cent fois plus que la servitude; ils te fuiraient avec effroi comme un fardeau prêt à les écraser" (Paris: Éd Garnier, 1962, 358–9).

26 The inscription by Simonides on the gravestone at Thermopylae, commemorating the last stand of Leonidas and his Spartans against the Persians, says it with the economy of perfect eloquence: "O stranger, go tell the Spartans that here, obedient to their edicts, we lie."

27 Some of the reasons for the continued force of nationalism, particularly linguistic, I discuss in my article "Why Do Nations Have to Becomes States?" in *Philosophers Look at Confederation,* ed. by Stanley French (Ottawa: Canadian Philosophical Association, 1978).

28 Ibid.

29 This same understanding conditioned the terms in which the independence issue was recently argued in Quebec. Nobody within the society questioned the right of the community to decide, or the propriety of its making a decision as a community, to stay in or get out of the larger union. Very wisely the leaders of federal parties conceded this point of "self-determination"; the issue was then argued out exclusively on the merits of secession.

30 This incident was described in an earlier draft of his memoirs but does not seem to have been included in the final published version: David Lewis, *The Good Fight* (Toronto: Macmillan, 1981).

31 This congruence is itself the result of a remarkable evolution in "English" Canada over the last century, during which its ethnic identification as British has steadily given way to a multicultural political identity. See the description of this in Kenneth McNaught, "The National Outlook of English-speaking Canadians," in *Nationalism in Canada*, ed. Peter Russell (Toronto: McGraw-Hill, 1966), 61–71. McNaught even makes the (perhaps overstated) claim that "the English-speaking view has always anticipated a Canadian nationality in which the significance of racial origin will diminish rather than increase" (63–4).

32 For instance, the turnout in Ontario for the federal elections of 1979 and 1980 was, respectively, 78 and 72 per cent, while the provincial turnout in 1977 and 1982 was, respectively, 65.6 and 58 per cent. In Quebec, the participation in the two federal elections was, respectively, 76 and 68 per cent, while that in the provincial election of 1976 was 85 per cent, and, in 1981, 82.52 per cent. The corresponding figures for Saskatchewan were federally 79 and 71 per cent, respectively, and 79.4 per cent (provincial election 1978) and 83.9 per cent (provincial election 1982).

33 Thus, the move towards centralization which, beginning in the Depression and acquiring intellectual definition from the Rowell-Sirois Report, accelerated during the war and carried well into the postwar period but was substantially rolled back after 1960 by a renewed assertion of provincial powers.

34 For instance, in 1981, U.S. government expenditure on all levels broke down in the following way: federal government, $719 billion; state governments, $292 billion; local governments, $289 billion (source: *National Data Book and Guide to Sources, Statistical Abstract of the United States, 1984*, 104th ed., U.S. Department of Commerce,

Bureau of Statistics, table 452). The corresponding figures for
Canada in 1983 were: federal, $93 billion, provincial, $82 billion;
local, $30 billion (source: Statistics Canada, *National Income and
Expenditure Accounts, 1st quarter 1984,* cat. no. 13–001, table 6).

35 For a discussion of our federal system from this strongly centralist
standpoint, see Garth Stevenson, *Unfulfilled Union* (Toronto: Macmillan, 1979). In general this book is a good antidote to this chapter,
since Stevenson tends to dismiss appeals to regional identity as
being manufactured by politicians for purposes of their own empire
building, or even more, at the behest of business and other economic interests, who have been generally concerned with limiting
government action, particularly when it is redistributive in effect. I
think this approach is deeply misguided, but it expresses one of the
(at present irreconcilable) attitudes which we have yet to bring to
some synthesis if we are ever to have an agreed formula of national
identity.

36 See Donald V. Smiley, *The Canadian Political Nationality* (Toronto:
Methuen, 1967), esp. 128–35.

37 This thesis may be challenged, that greater participation in a society
like ours generally requires decentralization on the grounds that
people can participate at all levels of self-government and the ideal
society would be one in which they did so maximally at all levels. In
principle this is undoubtedly true. But in practice, in a number of
domains, centralized solutions prevent or hamper local variation and
hence initiative, and thus intensify the sense that government is of
its essence distant, unresponsive, and bureaucratic. As an example,
draining power from local school boards to a provincial ministry of
education has frequently had this effect. There may be no concep-
tual link between participation and decentralization, but there is
often a strong empirical one.

Of course, this insight might be the basis for another criticism of
my main thesis in this chapter. Why be concerned for the power of
provincial governments? it might be argued. Why not decentralize
further to truly local communities? I am very sympathetic to this
move if it can be done. But a successful devolution of power presupposes that people identify with the community on which responsibility devolves. It is not sufficient to note that the people of a given
area, say, have common interests or common problems. Unless governing themselves as a unit means something important to them,

the institutions of self-rule remain without life, as testified by the appallingly low rate of voter participation in some local governments. This has been one of the major themes of my chapter. Historical community identification is a crucial condition of participatory politics. That is why the provinces constitute a crucial level in Canada, whether we like it or not.

38 For a good discussion of the harmful mutual stultification that can result from provincial rivalry, see Stevenson, *Unfulfilled Nation*, chap. 5.

39 From "Patmos": "But where danger threatens / That which saves from it also grows" (Michael Hamburger translation).

CHAPTER FIVE

Institutions in National Life

The following text was written for delivery at a conference celebrating the fiftieth anniversary of Laval University's Faculty of Social Sciences, which took place in Quebec City, 12 to 14 October 1988. In the absence of Charles Taylor, who was unable to attend, Vincent Lemieux read the paper. This conference on Quebec institutions was marked by a generalized feeling of uncertainty, which was caused by phenomena connected, in Taylor's view, with the constitutive malaise of modernity: exacerbation of individualism, predominance of instrumental rationality, and bureaucratization carried to extremes. Taylor's text presents the risks run by a society such as Quebec when its public institutions are reduced to the level of instruments so that they lose their meaning in the construction of individual and collective identity. Written before the derailment of the Meech Lake Accord and the opening of another great political-constitutional debate, this text nonetheless proposes a pluralistic ethics serving as a guide in deliberations on the future of Quebec as a national community.

WHAT IS AN INSTITUTION? JUST ABOUT EVERYTHING, it seems, and anything at all. In the language of sociologists, the family is an institution; so are trade unions and hospitals; retail businesses, service stations, the lottery, and junior hockey are too, just to mention a few. Faced with such diversity, undertaking the task of speaking about the foundation of the institution as such fills me with dread. I would prefer to carve out a small problem, to enclose

Translated from the French by Paul Leduc Browne

myself in a less extensive field. What I would like to talk to you about here is the way institutions fit into the life of a society – or, rather, the different ways in which they may do so, and the greatly varying meanings they can consequently have. This is not a very simple problem either, as you will see, and I shall only touch upon it, but I hope to be able to put forward some ideas that might provide the basis for a potentially fruitful discussion.

What is an institution? It is a very large and fuzzy phenomenon. We may speak of an institution every time the practice of a given population stabilizes around certain forms. Certain ways of acting become "normal" and often normative as well. These more or less regularized forms define different roles, and the members of a society begin to recognize themselves in these roles and consequently to assign obligations to themselves. It is at this minimal level of formalization that the family is an institution in every human society, even where it is not yet regulated by a legal code.

Beyond this first level, formalization can develop through different stages. The rules or norms of practice can be expressed or articulated instead of remaining unspoken. They can be enshrined in a code and imposed with the full force of all of society; or institutions can be more or less elaborate, involving a diversification of roles, or they can be more or less hierarchical, and so on. The average citizen, lacking experience in the language of social sciences, speaks of institutions only with regard to hierarchical structures recognized by law and would find it strange, if not sinister, to include the family in this category, not to mention junior hockey. Nevertheless, for the sake of my discussion, I shall hold to this expanded category.

We thus see this enormous range spreading out before us, from the family through hospitals, trade unions, and the Quebec government, all the way to service stations. All these are our institutions. We vaguely feel that they contribute to the shaping of our society, and so they do. But the way in which they contribute differs greatly from one to the next, and that is precisely what I would like to explore here.

TWO IDEAL TYPES OF INSTITUTION

The family and service stations represent the two extreme paradigms. Let us take service stations first. Ask anybody in our society to specify their meaning; it will always be defined in utilitarian and instrumental terms. These institutions have a well-defined function; namely, to provide a certain service. We use them without giving the matter too much thought, and often even without any human contact with those who work in them. For example, the legal norms that govern their working are a response to considerations of a utilitarian order or are put forward in order to avoid certain ills, such as exploitation or pollution, which can arise in the course of their operation. This is the paradigm of what I shall call service institutions.

Let us now take the family. It is something completely different. We are acutely conscious of this, precisely because our family is subject to rapid and sometimes bewildering changes, and some of us experience these as crises. The reason for this is that the different roles and norms connected with the family do not define external behaviour only, as is the case with service stations. As the years go by, the identity of each of the participants crystallizes in the relationship between husband and wife, between parents and children. These are exchanges that shape each of those who enter into them. It follows that to accept a certain norm of family life is to recognize a certain form of identity as valid. If I consent to be a father according to a certain model of family life, I take on by that very token a certain definition of myself.

My identity is a moral reality, which is to say that what I define myself in regard to are always normative views of life, conceptions of human life that have moral value. A role that contributes to moulding my identity thus necessarily comprises a vision of human life, an intuition of what is good or bad, of what is admirable or to be despised. Therefore, a role (and the practice in which it is embedded) can define good and evil for me, the good life or life without value, even apart from any articulation of it in terms of rules or principles or verbal descriptions. I live out a role within a practice; I share with others the sense of what is to be done and what is to be avoided. Things can remain thus, without our having to formulate rules or give a name to the different virtues and vices inherent in that practice. We would still have defined, on the strength of that very practice, a certain vision of life, with its implicit norms and morals.

It is often thus in family life. Yes, there are norms and models, recognized images of the family. But even where partners wish to hold to a recognized form, each family will have its own manner of living it, which in richness and concreteness will extend beyond generally accepted ways but will gain definition with the passing years through daily, often non-verbal exchanges.

With its implicit normativity, a practice can thus embody a moral standard or an ideal. It can constitute the first definition of this morality, there being no verbal definition, or the latter being much less and concrete than lived morality. What emerges from this discussion is the ideal type of an institution as formalization of a practice that will be the site of such a primary definition. The institution is not the point of application of a morality defined elsewhere; rather, it is the primary environment in which this morality gets elaborated; and as the first vehicle of this vision of life, it constitutes an important pole of identification for those who participate in it. It is the ideal type that is realized to a very high degree in the family, and this is what places it poles apart from the service institutions I defined above.

The contrast between these two ideal types, in the Weberian sense, constitutes the backdrop of my discussion. On the one hand, there are structures that have a merely instrumental relation to our lives, even if the service they supply is very important; on the other hand, there are environments characterized by practices that are the primary sites in which we define important values and hence the possible poles of identity. We may speak of institutions that serve versus institutions that identify. All are institutions of our society, but the respective ways they fit into our lives are very different.

We are obviously dealing with ideal types – that is, not concrete realities but descriptions of features in their purest state. Clearly, each of the paradigmatic examples I have chosen relates to its respective type, but most institutions are located in the middle. Indeed, they are a mixture of the two: in some ways, closer to service institutions; in others, closer to structures of identification. In addition, these paradigms are necessarily located close to their respective extremes. It is hard to imagine a service station's playing a role of identification in our lives (unless, perhaps, one is the proprietor, the heir to a whole line of garage owners), while a service family is a nightmare rather than a social category, a reproach that people hurl at each other as they break up, not a viable form.

Most institutions can move along the spectrum between these extremes. Their significance may reside more or less in their function of identification; or, conversely, they may slide in the direction of pure service structures. Moreover, this variation can become relative: institutions can take on a meaning as structures of identification for some and be experienced as mere instruments by others. These variations of a range of institutions between extremes are precisely what is significant for the life of a society.

There is an influential conception of modernization which makes it consist in part of institutions sliding towards the service side. In premodern societies the different political, economic, and social structures are imbued with moral and religious meaning. For example, a monarchistic state is conceived as the realization of a cosmic order. Many functions (in the areas of health or education, for example) are secured by institutions that come under either the state or the church. Modernization, accompanied by secularization, strips the state of its sacred aura, replaces religious institutions with secular structures, and is more and more preoccupied with their productivity. At the same time, society diversifies; religious and ideological pluralism intensifies. Traditional institutions can no longer have the same meaning for everybody. The second type of variation mentioned above is felt more and more; certain structures retain their meaning for some people as forms that constitute identity while, for others, they become simply dispensers of services.

According to this model of modernization, this movement is destined to find a new equilibrium within a pluralistic secular state. This balance is defined around a new division of functions. The institutions that retain a dimension pertaining to identification are supposed to be "private"; membership in them is voluntary, and they are not at all (or, at most, very loosely) tied to public power. In contrast, "public" institutions become service structures, which are sometimes very important, even essential, but are nevertheless devoid of any dimension pertaining to identification.

This schema is sometimes presented as a portrait of the mature modern state and sometimes as a norm to be attained. As a portrait, it does comprise many genuine features. Over the last few centuries, the institutions of Western society have definitely moved away from their function of identification. Our societies are undoubtedly becoming more and more pluralistic. One need only think of such formerly homogeneous nations as France and Germany. They not only include Catholics, Protestants, Jews, and non-believers in their ranks, but they also have a significant Moslem minority. This has not come about without producing tensions, but it is obvious that it cannot be reversed – except by a political and cultural catastrophe similar to that of the 1930s.

This portrait seems less faithful when it comes to the state. From the viewpoint of a certain influential theory, the state, too, is a service institution. Its function is to "allocate values."[1] It is to be regarded as a conversion mechanism, which takes the "demands" of its different members as inputs and which produces as outputs decisions that satisfy a set of these demands – ideally, the richest and most balanced set that can be achieved.

This analysis neglects a cardinal dimension of modern politics – that the modern state is generally a nation-state. Whether the nation is defined by language, culture, or political forms, patriotism plays an important role in the politics of nation-states, and one might even believe that they could not maintain their cohesion as liberal states if this were not so. If a majority of citizens really adopted a cool attitude towards a free state, treating it as a super-service-institution, that state would be in imminent danger of disintegration. Where patriotism – in other words, nationalist feeling – remains an integral part of a state's political culture (as is the case with most modern states, including Quebec, of course), political structures retain an indelible dimension as forms that constitute identity.

This conception of the neutralized state can also reappear as an ideal. There is a certain conception of liberalism, much discussed in the United States nowadays, which demands that the state be neutral with regard to the different conceptions of the good life that its citizens might espouse. The reasoning is not difficult to grasp. In an irremediably pluralistic society, a state that identifies with a certain conception of life will favour some people at the expense of others. A Christian state puts its Jewish and Moslem citizens at a disadvantage. The values that the state embodies must therefore be exclusively procedural; they must define the rules of justice – but not substantive morality.[2]

It must be said that neutrality seems no more realistic as an ideal than it was as a description, and partly for the same reasons. It is difficult to conceive of a democratic state that would really be devoid of any dimension pertaining to identification. It is clear, at least in our society, that one cannot conceive of a Quebec state that would not be called on to defend and promote French language and culture, whatever the diversity of our population.

This equilibrium model, in which political structures would be only instrumental, is therefore unrealistic. But it would provide the answer to a problem that remains: how to reconcile the needs of identification with the deep slide of modern pluralistic society towards the reduction of public structures to service institutions. Let us briefly examine the evolution of our society in this respect.

QUEBEC'S POLITICAL HISTORY IN PERSPECTIVE

During the last half-century, our society has followed a path of development that is related in some of its features to the portrait of modernization sketched above. A people who defined themselves by their language, and in the past also by religion, and who were subjected to strong pressures in North America left it up to their institutions not only to supply them with services but also to defend – and, at the same time, define – their identity. In the straitjacket of institutions constituting identity there was first of all the church, of course, whose very calling was poles apart from that of the service structures. A good many institutions which in other societies were already being treated as service structures (in the areas of education and health, for example) were here in the bosom of the church. Still others, such as the Caisses populaires and Catholic labour unions, were tied to the church in a less direct, more tenuous but still very real way.

One must not speak only of clericalism in this context. Some of these organizations were not managed by the clergy at all. The osmosis between church and institutions was also facilitated by national feeling. Indeed, one had the feeling that these structures were not only offering a concrete service but were building and defending national identity. Even people who were not part of them, who did not benefit from them, could identify with them on this account. Let us take the case of the Caisses populaires. A diffuse feeling of pride at this national achievement pervaded the French-Canadian society of the time, even beyond the movement's members. This is that much easier to understand nowadays since this feeling is far from dead. In the context of their position as structures of identification, it was not abnormal that these institutions should associate with the church, the prime gatherer of the nation in those days.

Similarly, one should not view the dissociation that has since occurred as being the effect of secularization alone. Secularization has had an effect, of course. There is no longer a gathering place, and attempts to build one now take place on the political level – I shall return to this later. But the same developments that elsewhere brought atomization, diversification, and the anonymity of big cities have had an effect on us too; they have tended to induce us to treat more and more as service structures the institutions that see to our needs.

All this has taken place simultaneously. Economic development and urbanization have contributed to creating the distances, the "dropping out" of community life, that have been observed elsewhere. The media have made us more open to other influences, and above all to American mass culture, which takes atomized society as its implicit backdrop. Dechristianization has made us more diversified, and now the growing percentage of francophone Quebeckers with roots abroad is only intensifying this diversity. All of this means, to take a particular example, that the percentage of people with Quebec roots using Sainte-Justine Hospital has diminished a lot over the last fifty years.

We have thus followed an evolution which, in many respects, parallels that which should lead to the neutral state, according to liberal theory. But we know that we cannot accept that final stop. We shall not be able to confine the identificatory function only to "private" institutions, families, and churches, now bereft of any mission of gathering the collectivity together. The function of identification cannot be excluded from the public domain, for the need to defend and redefine a national identity is still being felt – the same need that in bygone days caused institutions with a strong national vocation to be created. If the majority of institutions catering to our needs increasingly become service institutions, if their national vocation weakens in our eyes, then the work of self-definition will have to shift elsewhere; for it cannot possibly cease.

This shift is in fact taking place. The area where this work is more or less exclusively concentrated is the political arena. The political arena has always played an important role, but it is now bearing the entire load, which was previously more broadly distributed among a range of structures. This may be the reason for the intensification of political disagreements that has marked the latter phase of Quebec politics.

I have just mentioned a shift, but clearly this is not the only factor. What unfolded in the past through a wide range of institutions is not exactly the same process as that which nowadays is relatively concentrated in the political arena. On the contrary, the whole economy of national life is affected by it. It is a slow transformation and one that is difficult to grasp. Nevertheless, I shall try (perhaps uncautiously) to define it by sketching its broad outlines, with a bit of exaggeration to bring out the contrasts.

NATIONAL IDENTITY BEYOND UNANIMITY

I believe that the most striking contrast is the following one: in the past, the labour of self-definition unfolded under the sign of presumed unanimity. The French-Canadian and Catholic nation was in essence unanimous with regard to its faith and shared an unchallenged national goal. Obviously, I am speaking not of empirical reality but of shared self-description – of myth, if you will. But myths are part of social reality, and their contribution to that reality is not to be neglected.

There were thus important differences, which to some extent were legitimized as strategic differences with regard to the same ends; but the depth of the differences must often have been masked by recognized forms. For example, there was an opposition which, if it was not anticlerical, at least wanted to put some distance between church and state. This presented itself as another survival strategy for the Franco-Catholic community. Sometimes this was a disguise for unbelief, but the latter's legitimacy was not yet established.

This presumption of unanimity provided the framework for the institutions with a national vocation which I described above. It gave meaning to the notion of a "gathering" institution. The first of these institutions, which enjoyed unparalleled status, was naturally the church, because everybody, in essence, belonged to it.

But this same climate of profound agreement created a space in which other institutions could discharge a recognized national role, even though they were composed of only segments of the population. This was true of the Caisses populaires. But one could also conceive of an organization whose prime vocation was to gather the nation together, but which was the work of active minorities. I am thinking of the Société Saint-Jean-Baptiste. In referring to the society in the past tense, I am not suggesting that it no longer exists. I know that it is still alive and indeed is very active in certain parts of the province. My intention is merely to make explicit the unspoken presuppositions of a "patriotic" organization such as this, which in its own eyes enjoys a sort of *pars pro toto* status, that of herald of the nation, while assembling only a tiny part of the nation under its banner.

Now, I claim that these presuppositions no longer hold. We can no longer take the presumption of unanimity as our starting point. First, urban experience has to a certain extent atomized us; many of us, that is to say, no longer have close ties with our neighbours or with any local group. We feel family ties and are conscious of being Quebeckers, but the living cells, which formerly were the parish or village or even the neighbourhood, no longer mean anything to us. Dechristianization has contributed to this process by emptying parish churches. But it has also made us more diversified. It has undermined the prime ground of unanimity of bygone days – denominational unity. At the same time, the francophone population of Quebec has continually become more and more diversified by recruiting immigrants from all races, all religions, and all parts of the globe.

In these conditions, we can no longer take national identity for granted – as a given, as something already defined. This is all the more reason why we cannot consider it a source of unchallenged ends in which all recognize themselves *a priori*. This identity and these ends will henceforth have to be defined, negotiated, on the basis of outlooks that will be diverse and difficult to reconcile. In this context, the very idea of an association that claims to act as a gathering place in the name of everyone no longer has a meaning. Our starting point is different. How should it be described?

Not everything has changed. The feeling of national belonging remains. It is stronger than ever. But it is no longer linked *a priori* to a certain vision of things. We have taken a big step in the direction of the model of liberal society that I outlined above. We follow an irreducible multiplicity of visions. On what terrain does the nation find unity? Its ground is no longer defined according to a concrete content; instead, it is defined by the fact that everybody is attached to that identity in his or her own fashion, that everybody wants to continue that history and proposes to make that community progress. Unity is what one quarrels over; it is the hub of controversy.

It is because identity is now to be negotiated that the work of self-definition is shifting towards the political domain. But this transfer involves a qualitative change, and that is what I am trying to pinpoint here. It is not as if this identity became uncertain for a time, as if the ground of agreement rocked for a moment, to be firmed up again afterwards, thanks to political work. There is no going back, either to the unanimity of yesteryear or to a substitute that would fulfil the same function. This was the mistake of some followers of the Parti Québécois, who saw the organization as a potential gathering place that could give us back unchallenged common goals. They were right to see that the work of gathering had to take place in the political arena, but I believe they were wrong in failing to appreciate that this sort of work is obsolete, that it no longer has a place among us. Obviously, I am not speaking of the Parti Québécois as such; I am referring to the vision that sustained some of its members. Like every contemporary Quebec institution, the party is the meeting place of several visions. Yet there was something worrying, something redolent of gatherings of long ago, in the choice of its name: Parti *Québécois*.

I maintain that the work of definition is now political, not in the minimal sense that lost unity should once and for all be re-established by an effort of political mobilization, but in a more profound, irreversible sense. The definition of the national identity of Quebeckers will not only be the outcome of a political process; it will in part be constituted by this process. That is to say, the nation's prime ground of agreement will be the fair and honest contest between different tendencies aspiring to determine the community's goals. In other words, everybody comes together unanimously around the fact that a fair and democratic struggle is being waged over the destiny of the people. An integral part of this identity, which is in a perpetual process of redefinition, will consist of a certain conception of politics, a conception with deep Aristotelian roots, by the way, which attributes a more than instrumental value to politics as the way of life of free citizens.

To correct the lack of balance in my critique, I hasten to add that if this new conception of politics is dawning on our horizon, it is largely thanks to the Parti Québécois and its first leader, René Lévesque. In launching the project of independence, in thus placing themselves outside the old consensus, they enjoined us to make a very important choice about the form and future of our community. There are two ways of viewing this choice, and they correspond to what in my opinion are the good and bad sides of the Parti Québécois. One can see it as a choice between two interpretations of a national will, which is already inscribed in history. In this case, each option would treat the other as an aberration and would be in its rights in doing so. (Speaking of this, a good number of independentists were arguing, during the referendum of 1980, that the No supporters could not be true Québécois.) On the other hand, it can be seen as the confrontation of two visions, which at bottom are both legitimate but one or the other of which is considered to offer better chances for the survival or full development of the nation. The second outlook alone is compatible with the new role of politics in a post-unanimist national life.

There was a theme that kept recurring in the appraisals of René Lévesque under the shock of his sudden death in November 1987. It was his sense of democracy. What people were driving at, I believe, was, among other things, this sense of the legitimacy of multiple options. It is not only a generational question, for this is a lesson that has yet to be learned by the young people who booed certain non-independentist politicians during Félix Leclerc's funeral.

I said earlier that I was going to exaggerate a bit, and I see that I have kept my promise. I have slipped again into outlining ideal types. The unanimism of yesteryear was far from being without rifts, and we have not yet reached the degree of diversity that I am attributing to comtemporary Quebec. Where the real world involves tendencies, I have constructed pure instances. The mistake, if there is one, is to have anticipated a more or less ineluctable future. If that is true, my ideal types will perhaps prove to be revealing.

To sum up, after this slightly too circuitous discussion, I presented two groups of ideal types. First, I attempted to distinguish between two sorts of institutions, in keeping with their respective ways of fitting into social life: institutions that serve and institutions that identify. I took advantage of this to define a gamut of possibilities of social life according to the way the institutions fitted in. Modernization can be construed as an evolution towards an equilibrium in which most "public" institutions are service structures. I maintain that our society has followed an evolution that resembles this model, except that we could not possibly reach the outcome set by a liberal theory that is widespread in our time, because the political domain must remain the site of an important work of self-definition. I even claim that the role of the political increases by the very fact that other institutions lose their function of identification. But we are not speaking of a mere displacement; there is a transformation in the kind of work of self-definition that goes on. In fact, we have a new economy of national life and a new corresponding balance between institutions. This is where I launch my second group of ideal types: on the one hand, a national life presuming unanimity, in which many institutions with restricted recruitment can nevertheless construe themselves as having a national calling; on the other hand, a national life founded on diversity, in which the political process takes on a crucial significance, not only as an instrument of self-definition but as a major component of a national identity, which is largely constituted by debate, without definitive closure, between a plurality of legitimate options.

These options are many and are at several levels. I do not claim to compile an inventory of them here, but certain major strands stand out. First, there is the debate between federalists and independentists over the issue of constitutional status. The independentists seem to have lost some ground in the field of public opinion in recent years, but this is probably a temporary setback. Even if independentism in its classic form does not return in strength, we will continue to ask ourselves questions about our constitutional status and about our relationship with the other political entities that share this continent.

After this, we confront fundamental choices (analogous to those of other modern nations) with regard to how society is to be understood, built, and reproduced. Like all Atlantic nations, we are torn between, on the one hand, the demands of a mixed economy, which reserves an important place for markets, and, on the other hand, the conditions of social solidarity and community life. Like all those countries, we will not find a magic formula to overcome the dilemmas and tensions between these two kinds of demands – the pressures of international competition enjoining us to worry about efficiency, while the threats to the quality of our social life forbid us to neglect our community relations. In the final analysis, perhaps only more or less lame compromises are available in this area, but each society must find the path that suits it – and this is an invitation to a debate without closure.

In connection with these questions, we shall have to reconcile the demands within our political life for efficient management of the state with those philosophical debates in which fundamental projects are at stake; for a modern state is, among other things, a collective instrument for promoting individual ends. On this score, liberal theory is right to a certain extent. The point is to prevent the state from being only that, because the instant it becomes reduced to a merely instrumental role, our state will no longer be the site of a national life that is still active; it will have lost its function of self-definition completely. Reconciling instrumental efficiency and living exchanges is a difficult rask that is resistant to definitive solutions – and this opens another field of differences of opinion to be debated endlessly.

All of this makes us sensitive to the role filled by social philosophy in our social life. I am referring not only to the great universal doctrines: liberalism, socialism, and the like. On their own, they are likely to do us more harm than good; for, like all small countries, we have a tendency to take them over as they are from the hegemonic societies that elaborated them, even if they do not suit us at all. No, I am referring to social thought, which blends these great currents with a social imagination that is sensitive to our particularity and which is thus able to answer these universal problems with solutions that are truly made to measure for us.

Notes

1 See David Easton, *A Systems Analysis of Political Life* (New York: Wiley, 1965).
2 See, for example, John Rawls, *A Theory of Justice* (Cambridge, Mass.: Harvard University Press, 1971), and "Justice as Fairness: Political Not Metaphysical," *Philosophy and Public Affairs* 14, no. 3 (1985): 223–54; and Ronald Dworkin, "Liberalism," in *Public and Private Morality*, ed. Stuart Hampshire (Cambridge: Cambridge University Press, 1978).

CHAPTER SIX

The Tradition of a Situation

This chapter takes up some notes that Charles Taylor prepared for participation in a colloquium commemorating both the twentieth anniversary
of André Laurendeau's death and the founding of the Collèges d'en-
seignement général et professionnel (CEGEPS). The conference, which
took place at André-Laurendeau CEGEP in Montreal, 3 to 5 November
1988, set the scene for reflection both on the man himself and on education. Taylor's speech took its cue from Fernand Dumont, who empha-
sized Laurendeau's exemplary status in Quebec's intellectual life as
someone able to marry rootedness and universal pursuits. To Dumont's
question "Is there an intellectual tradition in Quebec?", Taylor answers
that Quebec intellectuals should first and foremost cherish the tradition
of their situation. Although this text is short compared with others in
this collection, it has been included because, for once, Charles Taylor
presents the origins of his own development. Furthermore, his remarks
on the universality of particularism are surprisingly topical in a world in
which some people think they once and for all hold the meaning of liberal justice, and in which others are already proclaiming the end of history. In the current debate, Taylor's remarks on the dangers of a *tabula
rasa* and of spurious universalism are aimed just as much at the zealots of
federalism as at the extremists of nationalism – in Canada as in Quebec.

Translated from the French by Paul Leduc Browne. Taken from *Penser l'éducation: Nouveaux
dialogues avec André Laurendeau*, ed. Nadine Pirotte (Montreal: Boréal, 1988).

FIRST OF ALL, I WOULD LIKE TO MAKE IT CLEAR that I do not feel at all qualified to speak about the Quebec intellectual tradition (though this is perhaps exactly why I have been invited to tackle the question). I do not feel qualified because, by virtue of my education, I feel eccentric with regard to that tradition. I earned my first university degree from McGill in the 1950s at a time when that institution was in a way detached from the Quebec context. After that, I studied abroad: in France, in England, in Germany. Thus, while there was a Quebec intellectual tradition, I was, so to speak, not acquainted with it.

Nonetheless, Fernand Dumont's distinction between intellectual tradition and tradition of the intellectuals seems important to me, and I believe that if one wishes to speak of an intellectual tradition in the sense that certain ideas are transmitted from father to son, from supervisor to student, from mentor to disciple, especially in the human sciences, then one should emphasize breaks more than continuity. In contrast, the tradition of the intellectuals refers to certain situations, certain problems, a certain continuity in life, with which all of those who think are faced, and from which their thinking must depart. In this regard, I can share my own experience with you. When I was a student in Europe, in a foreign country therefore, I felt a very strong affinity with Herder, the eighteenth-century German philosopher and one of the founders of modern nationalist thinking. Herder devoted much thought to language, the difference between languages, and the distortion in the thinking of a given language group when a language claims to be superior and better able to express universality, and when it therefore represses other languages. At the time, that language was French, which was invading the German intellectual world and was marginalizing German. In Herder I found inspiration, ideas that were very fruitful for me, precisely because I was from here. I was able to understand him from the situation I had experienced outside school, outside university, and I was able to engage with his thought, internalize it, and (I hope) make something interesting out of it.

This shows that even though I was isolated in a way from the Quebec intellectual tradition, it was impossible for me not to situate myself in the tradition of Quebec intellectuals; that is, in a particular historical situation. This type of belonging is invaluable.

One cannot think in a truly fruitful way in the human sciences and philosophy if one is cut off from a situation such as this. Real problems confront human beings only in a global fashion, as a totality that must then be analysed. If one tries to cut oneself off from lived experience in order to reflect on it, one's thinking about it is bound to be withered, without depth or interest. This tradition is invaluable for intellectuals as well as for society (whose situation could not otherwise really be envisaged).

I believe that there are currently two threats to this tradition, to this continuity of situation. First, there is the fact that we are going through or have gone through a period, if not of revolution, at least of a widespread desire among young people for a break with the past – the religious past, to be sure, but also the political past, the social past, and so on. This is the reaction that marked the 1960s and 1970s. The danger in this attitude is that in the moment of reaction, in the movement of rejection (as healthy and necessary as it may be), it is not only the solutions of our precursors that are rejected but also the situation in which they lived. There is there- fore a breach in that sympathy, in that recognition of a similarity of situation with our precursors, which goes well beyond a dis- continuity in the area of solutions. It prevents us from situating ourselves in that tradition. I believe that the reason we are cele- brating André Laurendeau today is that, in many respects, we find in him an innovator, a reformer, who thus had to break with many things but without having wished to break with the tradition of the situation. He always felt that he was in continuity with the situation experienced by those who preceded him.

This is one of the aspects of Laurendeau that impressed me tremendously when he was alive, even if I did not understand it very well at the time. If he has once again become an exemplary intellectual for us, it is perhaps because, in wishing to rediscover this tradition, we are almost inevitably prompted to invoke him. I believe that this is the essential meaning of this conference. It also answers Denis Monière's question: if the tenth anniversary of Laurendeau's death was passed over but the twentieth was not forgotten, it is because in 1978 our break was still under way. It seemed then that our precursors had not only nothing to teach us in the matter of revolutions but also that we had nothing to draw from the situation in which they lived, from the problems they had to confront, from the emotions they felt. We sought to create a *tabula rasa*. I believe that we are beginning to feel the need to revive our tradition and that this is why André Laurendeau is becoming important once again.

In addition to the dangers of a break, in addition to the desire for a renewal which, as it were, encompasses not only solutions but also situations, there is another danger of which Fernand Dumont has spoken to us. This is the danger of spurious universalism or, as Dumont puts it, of generalization. Human sciences by their nature – by the way in which they came into being and in which they are constituted in our civilization (this can be seen in the very expression "human sciences") – have always tended towards what they call the universal but what is more precisely, in Dumont's terminology, the general. This means that human sciences seek absolute laws, which are everywhere and always valid, by bracketing out real differences. I have always opposed this way of seeing things, and in this I have drawn inspiration from Herder in particular. But when one does not even try to resist the desire to generalize, one is convinced that there is a solution somewhere, a truly adequate and universally valid form of thinking that can be found elsewhere – in Paris, in New York, in Cambridge ... We then think of ourselves as provincials chasing after magic recipes concocted in major centres. This is a constant danger, not only because it displays and reinforces an inferiority complex, but also because in succumbing to it one submits to "science's" logic of generalization.

There is indeed in the ideology of the human sciences the idea that a corpus of universal thoughts exists, to which one must adapt oneself. Throughout the development of the human sciences in Quebec, one finds a constant struggle, which is usually lost, for emancipation from the thoughtless hegemony of forms of thought that claim to be universal but bear the marks of a particular situation: present-day American sociology, the Parisian Neo-Nietzscheanism of the 1970s, and so on. To resist the seduction of the accredited answer, one must not only be able to tame the imitation reflex generated by our weakness as a people; one must also be able to swim against the current of the direction inherent in this form of science. I think that here, too, André Laurendeau can serve as an example for us in accomplishing this. I very much liked Fernand Dumont's statement that Laurendeau had discovered that we were very narrow, but without losing sight of the fact that great peoples are not bereft of this trait. It is precisely this ability that allows us to see, in the so-called universal thought emanating from Paris or New York, a reflection of the Fifth Republic of the 1970s or of the American republic's ideological sickness of the 1990s.

Besides, when one manages to understand the universality of particularism, one is cured of the illusion that we are eccentric. There are only eccentricities, there are only eccentric positions, ours among others. A genuine intellectual tradition may not yet exist among us, but that will come when it comes. What is important, on the other hand, is what I call the tradition of the situation, the tradition of the intellectuals. But it is always threatened. It is of the greatest importance for us, as intellectuals, and for our entire society. The danger of losing it comes both from the desire for rupture, which is often very justified but easily overshoots the mark, and from the magic, the illusion, of universal science. If we can continue fighting against these two major seductions, I believe that we have a good chance of maintaining this tradition with all of its potential fruitfulness for us.

CHAPTER SEVEN

The Stakes of Constitutional Reform

This chapter is a translation of the brief that Charles Taylor presented to the Commission on the Political and Constitutional Future of Quebec, 19 December 1990. About sixty experts answered a series of questions put to them by the Bélanger-Campeau Commission. Half of these people, including Charles Taylor, were invited to appear before the members of the commission to give an account of their thinking. In this brief, Taylor does not renounce his federalist convictions or the arguments contending that political integration with Canada is the road that Quebec must follow in future as a distinct society. On the other hand, he does not believe that any form of integration will do. To save federalism, Taylor believes, it is necessary to understand that the current Canadian constitution has, in a way, been morally defunct since the failure of the Meech Lake Accord. A mere make-up or patching-up job will not suffice. After the crisis, he suggested that the commission's members take advantage of the situation to define a new political contract between Quebec and Canada. There are hints in this text of the constitutional storm that swept over Quebec in the months following the failure of Meech.

THE CURRENT CONJUNCTURE OFFERS AN HISTORIC OPPORTUNITY. We are being invited to rethink our political and constitutional structure from top to bottom, and to do so without the constraints that accompanied the long-standing Canadian Constitution, whose

Translated from the French by Ruth Edwards Abbey

renewal was proving increasingly difficult. We can envisage Quebec, at least as a starting point for this reflection, as a society free of all previous commitments, which is preparing to give itself structures that suit it and which, as a consequence, is thinking of proposing to one or some possible partners new arrangements that would be of common interest.

How should these structures be imagined? I shall begin with an attempt to define the constitutional problem.

THE CONSTITUTIONAL PROBLEM

Quebec's constitutional problem can be summed up thus – how to reconcile the imperatives that flow from certain fundamental facts. I see four such facts:

1 Quebec is a distinct society, the political expression of a nation, and the great majority of this nation lives within its borders.
2 Quebec is the principal home of this nation, but branches of it have settled elsewhere in Canada and North America.
3 Quebec must open itself economically, as must any society that seeks prosperity at the end of the twentieth century.
4 This economic openness must not be bought at the cost of political domination from outside. This danger exists because we share the continent with a superpower. Quebec therefore has an interest in political association with the other regions of what is currently Canada in order to maintain a certain balance in North American political relations and to enjoy some weight internationally.

The difficulty of our previous situation arose from the fact that these demands were often viewed as conflicting. One could argue, for instance, that too unconditional a solidarity with the francophones outside Quebec – point (2) above – causing us to impose certain conditions on other provincial governments, could lead to the weakening of Quebec's constitutional position. Alternatively, the benefits of collaboration with the other regions – point (4) above – could be mitigated by the dangers of a political structure that did not adequately recognize and guarantee the distinct nature of Quebec.

In the face of these difficulties, some have preferred a radical option: the abandonment of some of these imperatives in favour of other, more fundamental ones. This is the independentist position, as it has generally been defended over the last twenty-five years. To safeguard the full autonomy of Quebec as a political entity – a demand flowing from (1) – and to maintain economic openness (3), what is proposed is the abandonment of all political ties with francophones outside Quebec (2) and of all the benefits of a wider political collaboration (4).

Since this would involve sacrificing some important benefits, we would have to be sure that it was really essential. Regarding francophones outside Quebec, it is not just a question of historical and cultural ties, though I do not want to minimize these. It is also necessary to take into account the fact that these communities represent the dissemination of French in North America. The stronger they are and the more they make themselves recognized in their respective provinces, the more do they enlarge the French presence. That is a great advantage for us in Quebec, who are at the heart of the Francophonie in America. The pressure on us is reduced when we are surrounded by a demographic and political space that is not homogenous or monolithic.

Political collaboration with the other regions also can contribute to this dissemination of French. The process of bilingualism in Canada, the growing number of English Canadians who are learning French, the sometimes extraordinary expansion of immersion schools – all this is an undeniable advantage for the Quebec Francophonie. Anything that enhances the prestige of French, that increases the number of people capable of communicating in French, diminishes the pressure that a minority language will always experience in North America.

These gains have been underestimated and insufficiently appreciated in Quebec thanks to the political context in which they were made. The Trudeau government was largely responsible for the growth of bilingualism, but it linked bilingualism's growth with a categorical refusal of special status for Quebec. Instead, bilingualism was defended in the name of a philosophy that relied on a rigorously symmetrical federalism. It was conceived of as an individual right of French and English speakers, and not as the recognition of a community, in this case francophone, that was forced to protect its survival and growth.

But this association is neither dictated by logic nor inscribed in fact. In André Laurendeau's vision, for example, federal bilingualism had to be paired with increased powers for Quebec. The internal logic of this combination of objectives was perfectly coherent. It began with the recognition of a French-Canadian nation being associated with another people in a federal structure. Such an association demanded the equality of the two languages in the federal institutions on the one hand and, on the other, a political status giving sole jurisdiction over certain matters where this nation was in the majority. Its status would not be that of one province among several in a symmetrical federalism.

The political dynamic of the Trudeau-Lévesque era has made us forget this program, a program that is both logical and profoundly in tune with our historical aspirations. For the last quarter of a century it has been passed off as utopian. We have felt compelled to choose between an anti-communitarian philosophy recognizing individual rights only, which was dominant in Ottawa, and an independentist strategy that gained ground in Quebec. It seemed that Quebec could only find the political status it needed at the expense of the spread of French outside its borders.

But this choice is not inevitable. We no longer have to remain obsessed by the political configuration of the last twenty-five years. That era is finished. With the process manifested in the Bélanger-Campeau Commission, we are starting a new phase. It is no longer a question of the dilemmas of a passing era. We want to define them for a future that is as yet undetermined. We do not have to restrict them from the start.

Apart from this question of the spread of French, there are further advantages from collaboration with the other regions of what is currently Canada that must be taken into account. Without claiming to offer an exhaustive list, I shall mention three.

The first is connected with the fact that Canada distinguishes itself from the United States by its social programs; for example, our old-age pensions and especially our health insurance. Canadians and Quebeckers hold these programs dear. But they are not necessarily given once and for all. Especially in the context of

North American free trade, there will always be a certain pressure on us to align our social spending and taxation levels with those of our powerful neighbour. The different provinces and regions of Canada have a common interest in not ceding to this pressure. There is an objective solidarity between them. We ought not to be indifferent to the fate of the other regions in this regard. To the extent that cooperation between the regions can support the maintenance of these programs, as has been the case for their equalization, it is in the interests of all, including Quebec.

Secondly, Quebec also differs from the United States, as well as from the Anglo-Saxon world in general, in its style of economic management. In Quebec the state plays a much more active role in the economy. We need only mention the important role of the Caisse de dépôt in our recent development. In this we resemble (not necessarily in detail of course, but in philosophy of economic growth) certain European countries, even Japan, more than our Anglo-Saxon neighbours. In this it is also important that we should not be forced to align ourselves with the United States. Canada has always offered a climate hospitable to this type of government intervention. For historical as much as geographical reasons, English Canada has always been much more open to such state initiatives than the United States has.

Moreover, it is to be hoped that the other regions of Canada and also any future federal government will adopt some of the measures that have contributed to Quebec's economic success. One of them, the generation of capital from citizens' savings, could enlarge the range of possibilities if practised more frequently and widely; it could permit the financing of large-scale projects or enterprises. One resource that is currently underutilized in Quebec and Canada is government-sponsored scientific research; here, too, the results could be much more significant if our efforts were united.

Finally, there is a very important reason for not withdrawing from the Canadian space to that behind our borders. It is because this space contains vast resources, some still unknown. Rather than being forced to retreat, we must aim to participate in the development of the northern half of this continent. The advantages of this participation in terms of factors and resources currently known cannot be expressed. The future wealth and opportunities of this vast area are in part unforeseeable. We cannot let ourselves be excluded from all this before it has even begun.

Consequently, it is necessary to take account of the four types of imperative outlined above. Of course, we must allow for the possibility that some of them will prove to be unrealizable in the face of the incomprehension or ill will of our negotiating partners. But there is no need to abandon them in advance.

We are now faced with an unprecedented opportunity to define ourselves. We will have to establish our optimal objectives while being ready to step back from them if need be. But above all, we must not, because of historical disappointments, limit the scope of our aspirations before we have even begun.

This is particularly true because the historical context of these disappointments is behind us. With the death of the Meech Lake Accord, something very profound happened in Quebec. Everybody feels it, but it is not easy to define. For me, the most significant element is that the long-felt ambiguity of the Quebec federalists has been resolved. I do not mean that they are no longer federalists. But the age-old uncertainty about the question of whether it was necessary to make certain changes to the 1867 Constitution or whether we had to remake our structures from head to foot has gone. On 23 June 1990, the 1867 Constitution died morally in Quebec. It is necessary to create anew. This is the reason for the deep feeling of relief, of gaiety, that all observers felt on Saint-Jean-Baptiste Day that year. It is the type of relief one feels when an ambivalence that has troubled one for a long time is finally resolved.

But to make anew means to start without the legacy of the old structures, without their limitations and dilemmas, and without being inhibited by the quarrels that were inseperable from them. We should not constrain this new exercise in self-definition because of the old reflexes.

Of course, it is quite possible that the old misunderstandings between Quebec and English Canada which destroyed the previous structures will survive, that they will plague the new relationships we want to establish. This is possible, but it is far from being inevitable. Some of these misunderstandings were tied up with the old constitution. The image of Canada as a "mosaic," the norm of the equality of the provinces, the *idée fixe* that there was only a "Canadian" nation – all these elements were tied to the existing structures and to the way in which those structures were explained and experienced in the other regions. Canada created a certain expectation in the minds of a majority of English Canadians – an expectation regarding the provinces and other parts of the country, which Quebec could not violate. The advantage of creating is that new structures, which break explicitly with past images, can be put forward. It will no longer be a question of treason against the essence of an existing Canada; it will be a matter of building a new country.

In other words, contrary to those who believe that English Canada, having refused Meech Lake, could not agree to bigger changes, there is a real possibility that deeper changes will be easier to accept insofar as they are proposed within the framework of a new constitution rather than as rearrangements of the old Canada. At least, this is the opinion of the experienced constitutionalist Alan Cairns of the University of British Columbia.

Of course, this requires that English Canada will take the same route and agree that the old constitution is defunct. Now, I admit that our compatriots are still far behind us in this regard. The Québécois know that English Canadians need to be alerted, to be sent a message. But two questions should be distinguished here: how to lead them to negotiate and what to propose to them once negotiations are under way. Some Québécois seem to lean towards extreme positions and to favour irreversible, unilateral moves in order to impress the seriousness of the matter upon their bargaining partners. But we should not have our objectives dictated by such tactical considerations. To put it differently, we do not have to determine our destination according to the difficulties of the itinerary.

The commission on the constitutional future of Quebec must formulate our objectives with the optimal situation for Quebec in mind and to this end should keep sight the four types of imperative I outlined above.

Of course, this assumes that we will find ways of encouraging our fellow citizens to redefine Canada with us. I shall return to this question in my discussion of process.

THE DISTRIBUTION OF POWERS

I come now to the constitutional structures and the division of powers. It seems to me the system that best meets the four types of demands would be a federal system more decentralized than the current one. The 1867 Constitution is very supple in certain regards. The proof is that it was conceived as a very centralist system but has evolved over recent decades to a more and more obvious decentralization. It would be necessary to tailor the system to fit some of the recent developments, especially to avoid the misunderstandings and false expectations that have done so much to sow division within contemporary Canada.

Quebec and – in the case of a symmetrical federation – the other members of the federation would have to keep their current provincial powers, plus a certain number of others, such as powers over labour, communications, agriculture, and fisheries (this is not a complete list). The federal state would control defence, external affairs, and currency. As well, there would be some areas of mixed jurisdiction, such as immigration, industrial policy (including scientific research), and environmental policy.

This distribution would put an end to some useless duplications of effort that we currently have, without avoiding all overlap, which would be impossible anyway. The fact is that we do not live in a vacuum and even certain fully provincial powers cannot be exercised without regard for what is being done outside. Take health insurance, for example. To maintain an open economy in Canada means being concerned with mobility. Our health insurance system is our business, but we have an interest in extending it to others. The same applies to retirement pensions, labour policy, and many other domains.

In some cases, coordination will occur through interprovincial agreements, but in others it would be better to imagine a shared or concurrent jurisdiction. We could exercise shared power in the case of immigration, for example, because the free movement of people within the federation requires a regime that is accepted by both levels. We could also exercise concurrent power in a domain such as scientific research, because here our problem is not an excess of initiatives but a shortage of public funds.

As for ecology, some very obvious coordination problems exist. Regulation by intergovernmental agreements may be possible, as is currently the case between Canada and the United States with regard to acid rain and purification of the Great Lakes. But the size and urgency of these problems, and the magnitude of the changes that have to be made, push towards a mixed jurisdiction.

In a sense, even foreign affairs should be considered a mixed domain. Under the current regime, Quebec has developed an international identity for the matters under its jurisdiction, so the new structures will have to enshrine this capacity.

Another issue relating to the distribution of powers currently presents itself to all Canadians – the native question. I take it as given that its resolution requires the granting of certain powers of self-rule to aboriginal communities. One could imagine a purely Québécois solution for the Indians and Inuit of Quebec, leaving the other regions to legislate as they choose about communities within their territories. But there are clearly certain advantages to a common solution affecting all the native populations of the Canadian federation. In the first place, some tribes cross provincial boundaries; this is the case with the Mohawks, for example. But quite apart from such geographic considerations, two or more regimes would always invite comparisons, criticisms, and demands that could render the new structures unstable. It is important that the new structure of self-rule be given the fullest chance to succeed. We must go beyond dreaming about yesterday's structures so that today's problems can be addressed. To that end, a continent-wide regime would be far preferable.

One last point before I move on to examine the structures of the federation is that it would be good if the new regime could retain the best features of the current one, such as a system of equalization between the regions.

THE FEDERAL STRUCTURES

A federation uniting whom? Who would be Quebec's partners? Unfortunately, it is impossible to specify this at the moment. Moreover, it is not for us to decide. English Canada itself, once it has understood and accepted that the country has to be remade from top to toe, will determine its identity.

It is therefore necessary to examine several scenarios to measure their impact on the federal model outlined above. I rule out one possibility, a catastrophic scenario in which English Canada would disintegrate under the weight of its internal divisions as soon as it saw that the current structure would not hold. This is a possible but not probable outcome; but that is not my major reason for ruling it out. My reason is that such an outcome would leave us without a negotiating partner. I envisage three possibilities:

1 English Canada recovers its unity, either as a unitary state or a federation, and seeks to combine with Quebec in a federation of two.
2 English Canada takes account of its own regional differences and restructures itself under three or four regional governments, which would become Quebec's negotiating partners.
3 English Canada remains as it is, composed of nine provinces.

It is clear that the type of federal system would not be the same under all three hypotheses. Under (1), a perfectly symmetrical federalism can be envisaged, because it is obvious that a united English Canada would also push for a considerable decentralization of powers. Under (3), by contrast, it is more than probable that the system would be asymmetrical. This means that only Quebec would exercise fully the powers that I attributed above to all the members of the federation, while the other provinces would opt for the centralization of several powers. Hypothesis (2) would probably represent an in-between case. By this outcome the system would resemble symmetrical federalism, but there would possibly be minor differences in the powers that its different members would want to exercise.

In this uncertain context, I believe that Quebec should decide what powers it wants but should not try to dictate those of others. If the list of powers differed, it would be necessary to build a system of asymmetrical federalism. Under scenarios (2) and (3) it would even be advantageous to ensure flexibility of the division of powers. As well as an initially asymmetrical distribution – or maybe in its place – one could envisage the possibility of a delegation of powers from one level to another. English Canada could thus evolve towards greater decentralization or centralization according to its wishes and the needs of the time.

But is it as simple as this? Talk of asymmetrical federalism means special status for Quebec, and we all know how its very invocation provoked the resistance of English Canada and how dangerous it can seem to some of our compatriots. The rejection of such a status was an important feature of the opposition to the Meech Lake Accord. Yet we should not automatically assume that asymmetry is impossible or unworkable. The fact is that Quebec enjoys considerable special status under the current regime. We live every day with asymmetrical federalism. Quebec is the only province that raises its own taxes, has its own pension plans, is active in immigration, and so on. The big problem with Canada is its inability to recognize explicitly in its constitutional texts what it has been living as fact for a long time. This sums up what was at stake in the Meech clause recognizing Quebec as a distinct society. The resistance was not at the practical level, caused by concrete inconveniences. This may have been the case for some of the other clauses of the accord but not for this one.

This was rather a principled resistance, a defence of the principle of the equality of the provinces. It is as if we could tolerate considerable departures from this principle in fact as long as the principle was safely protected in texts. It is resistance at the level of feeling. This is not insignificant, of course, but the obstacles it creates should not be exaggerated. For one thing, the "distinct society" idea also has considerable support in English Canada. Furthermore, the resistance is linked, as I mentioned above, to certain expectations that the idea of Canada has traditionally created for some of our compatriots. It is a matter of convincing them that we are no longer playing the same game, that we are not proposing to repair the Canada of old. There must be a new deal.

But are there not still some very real difficulties in according one member a significant special status in a federal structure? The problem of federal parliamentary representatives is often cited in this regard. Let us take an area where power is accorded to province X but is exercised for the other provinces, Y and Z, by the federal government. When the federal parliament is deciding on a measure in this domain that affects provinces Y and Z, what should the deputies of X do? Should they abstain so as not to involve their constituents? Or should they vote like the others and open themselves to the accusation that their constituents have double power – that of deciding their own policies in this domain, through their provincial government, and also of participating through their federal deputies in determining the policies of the others? If the second option seems unfair, the first also has some inconveniences, especially in a parliamentary system in which the government can lose its majority if the deputies of a given region abstain.

In theory, this seems to be a serious obstacle to asymmetrical federalism, but in practice it is not necessarily so. To see this, let us look at a concrete example. In 1964 the scenario outlined above in algebraic terms occurred regarding the pension scheme. Ottawa and Quebec came to an agreement whereby Quebec would have its own program and the federal government would legislate for the rest of the country. No one suggested that the Quebec representatives in the House of Commons should withdraw from deliberations on this issue. In part this was because everyone recognized that this legislation also had repercussions for Quebec. It was essential that the two schemes be aligned to make portability possible. It was not a case of decisions being made in a vacuum, without one affecting the other.

But did Quebeckers not have two voices in this affair, deciding on their own scheme while at the same time having a say in the other? Yes they did, in a sense; and if Quebec constituted three quarters of Canada, that would be intolerable. But the opposite is true. A region that has a quarter of the economic and demographic power always experiences a certain unequal pressure when agreeing to develop uniform programs. (It should be noted that this pressure is not a function of the political regime. It also applies when two sovereign states negotiate.) The fact of being represented at the heart of your partner only redresses this asymmetry a little. Moreover, all the measures discussed in Parliament have repercussions for others. That is why it is not seen as shocking when representatives from the West participate in decisions about the Maritimes or when Maritime representatives vote on the wheat board.

I do not want to overstate this. Beyond a certain threshold, a federalism that is too asymmetrical would create problems. That is why the best scenario for us is probably scenario (2), in which English Canada forms itself into three or four large regions. Incidentally, this scenario is also superior to (1) for another reason: history shows that federations with two members are generally unstable. But we should no longer be led astray by theoricians – whether they be Quebec independentists or supporters of "One Canada" – who want to make us believe that asymmetry per se poses insuperable problems. Canada's own experience shows the contrary.

THE STATUS OF MINORITIES

I would like to mention briefly an arrangement that must involve a completely new federal pact. I am devoting a separate section to this because it is an agreement that we must try to realize even if all federal ties prove to be impossible. I am taking up an idea once advanced by René Lévesque, which was picked up again recently by the Quebec justice minister, Gil Rémillard.

The latter has spoken of a "code for minorities," but I do not insist on it being called this. Basically, the idea is that together we establish the principle, while recognizing that French will dominate in Quebec and English elsewhere, that linguistic minorities are not simply crushed. In other words, in each society, in Quebec and the rest of Canada, the minority language will enjoy a special status and will not be relegated to the level of another immigrant language.

We have three major reasons for wanting to make such an agreement. Firstly, by virtue of the imperatives of type (2), which I mentioned at the outset, our ties of solidarity and interest with the francophones outside Quebec push us towards it. Secondly, a mean-spirited and repressive policy towards minorities by one side or the other will poison relationships between the two societies, and good relations are important no matter what the political regime – federalism or sovereignty association. Thirdly, Quebec itself, through several of its leaders, including the premier and the leader of the opposition, has recently declared that it considers the anglophone minority to be a traditional and integral part of Quebec society.

What should the provisions of such an agreement be? I will not go into detail but would like to mention two things. First, the agreement should not provide the opportunity for a step backwards with regard to the often-fragile status of francophone communities outside Quebec. It may be necessary for the accord to ratify the principle that existing rights remain, while also securing objectives for a gradual improvement of the situation for relatively disadvantaged groups. Secondly, this agreement could provide the opportunity to destroy certain confusions that have poisoned our political life, and it could separate certain key issues in language policy. What are the powers that Quebec must reserve for itself in order to be able to defend or promote the French language? And what rights is Quebec prepared to give to its anglophone minority? What line is to be drawn between these two types of consideration?

CONSEQUENCES OF THE PROPOSED SOLUTION

As for our standard of living, I believe that a regime of the type proposed here would be the most favourable. In the first place, it would keep the Canadian economic space intact, and a federal regime offers a more stable framework that better guarantees the integrity of this space over the years. Secondly, a federal regime would be able to mobilize the resources of this vast country in the most efficient way, by promoting research and the concentration of capital at the most opportune level.

As for the Québécois identity, there are two things that must be asked from a constitutional structure: that it recognize fully and explicitly the specificity of Quebec, and that it give Quebec the powers necessary to defend and promote this uniqueness. I believe that the proposed federal structure adequately meets these two demands.

There are other important issues bearing upon the Québécois identity that do not relate to the constitutional framework that ties Quebec to the rest of Canada. I am thinking especially of the very definition of a Québécois in the popular awareness and of the challenge of multiculturalism that must be raised again. Our conception of francophone society in Quebec must move towards a more multi-ethnic model if it wants to adjust to the changing reality and to accord it the place it deserves. This is an important issue that should perhaps be taken into account in drawing up an internal Quebec constitution, but I am unable to pursue it here.

A CODA ON PROCESS

It may be tempting, as I indicated above, to try to decide questions of process with substantive propositions. Some want to convince English Canada of our seriousnees – and to lead it to negotiate – by taking extreme positions. Some people have even said that the only way to make English Canada negotiate seriously is to declare sovereignty first and bargain later.

I believe, however, that it is wrong to have our ultimate destination dictated by the difficulties encountered along the way. Therefore, we must find a means of alerting English Canada to the seriousness of the issue. We must avoid becoming embroiled in the maze of amendment procedures that currently exist. The problem with these procedures is that they leave us with the status quo by default. They put the burden of proof on those who want change. It may be necessary to propose to English Canada something like a rerun of the Charlottetown Conference of 1864 whose defeat would not leave us with the status quo but would signify the end of the country. In effect, it is an ultimatum that could take several forms, but I will not try to catalogue them here.

Such an ultimatum would have a shock effect, of course. This is probably necessary, given that English Canada is rather far behind Quebec in realizing how critical the condition of the country is. But a shock also risks damaging the interlocutor, leaving him or her less inclined to talk. It may therefore be useful to couple the ultimatum with an expression of openness, recognizing that Quebec is not alone in wanting to remake the country, that other regions have their own agendas, as we have ours, and declaring ourselves ready to listen to their demands just as we expect them to listen to ours.

In conclusion, it is up to us to decide what Quebec wants. But to achieve our goal, we must also take account of what the other side wants. Firmness need not mean closedness. At one determined and open, we can begin the political reconstruction of the northern part of this continent.

CHAPTER EIGHT

Shared and Divergent Values

As a political philosopher, Charles Taylor is one of the dominant figures in a debate that has raged for ten years or so in Anglo-American thought between the followers of liberal individualism and those who assign more value to citizens' particular roots. Taylor's communitarian sympathies come to the fore in this text, which was first presented during a study day organized by the Business Council on National Issues in January 1991 in Toronto. In it Taylor identifies the great trans-formations that have shaken the societies of Canada and Quebec during the last decades, as well as noting the reasons for the contemporary crisis. He believes that the Canadian vessel is threatened with ship-wreck on the shoals of "deep diversity" over the refusal to recognize the different senses of national belonging of English-speaking Cana-dians, Québécois, and aboriginal peoples. Taylor warns Canadians and Quebeckers that they are condemned to deliberating, together or sepa-rately, this question of the diversity of forms of belonging and collective identities.

ARE THERE DIVERGENCES OF VALUE between the different regions of Canada? In a sense, these are minimal. There appears to be a remarkable similarity throughout the country and across the French-English difference when it comes to the things in life that are important. Even when it comes to the values that specifically

Taken from *Options for a New Canada*, ed. Ronald L. Watts and Douglas M. Brown (Toronto: University of Toronto Press, 1991). Reprinted by permission of University of Toronto Press Incorporated.

relate to political culture, there seems to be broad agreement. About equality, non-discrimination, the rule of law, the mores of representative democracy, about social provision, about violence and firearms, and a host of other issues.

This was not always the case. Half a century ago, it seemed that there were serious differences between the two major groups as far as political culture was concerned. Pierre Trudeau wrote about this.[1] The ravages of Maurice Duplessis on the rule of law, which he seemed to be able to get away with – his treatment of Jehovah's Witnesses and Communists – seemed to indicate that Quebec and French Canada had different views about the toleration of dissent. Some people were ready to believe that the two societies gave quite different values to the maintenance of unity around certain cherished truths and standards when these conflicted with the goods of tolerance, freedom, or permitted diversity. Not that the rest-of-Canada was all that liberal in those days. Various minorities and dissidents had a rough time. But the particular grounds for illiberalism were rather strikingly different in Quebec, seemingly organized around the values of a traditional, ultramontane Catholicism. They made the province stand out as exotic and disturbing in the eyes of other Canadians.

This difference has disappeared today. Partly one might say that French Canada has rejoined "English" Canada; more accurately one might say that the forces within Quebec that were always striving for a liberal society have won out. Perhaps it would be more insightful to say that both parts of Canada have been swept up into the liberal consensus that has become established in the whole Western world in the wake of World War II. As we shall see below, some English-speaking Canadians still seem to doubt this, to harbour a suspicion of Quebec's liberal credentials. Such a suspicion is quite unfounded in the 1990s; or rather, suspicions are in order, but just as they are about any other Atlantic society, for none is exempt from racism, chauvinism, and similar ills.

Ironically, at the very moment when we agree upon so much, we are close to breakup. We have never been closer to breakup in our history, although our values have never been so uniform. The road to uniformity goes beyond the ironing out of differences between the two major cultures. There has also been a steady erosion of urban-rural differences in outlook over the last half-century. And the prodigious effect of modern communications has probably lessened all the various regional differences as well.

WHY CANADA?

So what is the problem? It emerges when you ask another kind of question, which also is in the realm of values in some broad sense. Not "What do people cherish as good?" but "What is a country for?" That is, what ought to be the basis of unity around which a sovereign political entity can be built? This is a strange question in a way; it is not one that would likely be asked in many countries. But it arises here because there are alternatives and therefore a felt need for justification. These alternatives exist for us – in our understanding of our situation – even when they are not very likely, when they enjoy minimal support and are hardly in the cards politically. They can still exist as a challenge to self-justification because they existed historically and we retain the sense that our existing arrangements emerge out of a choice that excluded them.

In Canada outside Quebec (COQ)[2] the alternatives have been two: the country or bits of it could join together or could join the United States; also, the bits might have failed to join together – or, having joined, might one day deconfederate. So there are two existential questions for COQ which we can call the unity and distinctness questions, respectively. For Quebec there is one big question, which is too familiar and too much on the agenda today to need much description. It is the issue of whether to be part of Canada or not; and if so, how. I stress that neither of the existential alternatives may be strong options in COQ today, but that does not stop them functioning as reference points for self-definition, as ways of defining the question "What do we exist for?" In a sense, the existential questions of the two societies are interwoven. Perhaps COQ would not feel the need for self-definition – for an answer to the question "What is Canada for?" – to anything like the same degree if Quebec was not contemplating answering its existential question in a radical form. But once the country's existence is threatened in this way, all the suppressed alternatives rise to the surface in the rest of Canada as well.

So what are the answers? It will be easier to set out the problem by taking "English" Canada first. The answer here used to be simple. Way back when it really fitted into our official name of British North America, the distinctness question answered itself; and unity seemed to be the corollary of the drive for distinctness in face of the American colossus. But as the Britishness, even "Englishness," of non-Quebec Canada declines, this becomes less and less viable as an answer. We are all the Queen's subjects, but this seems to mean less to fewer people; and, more awkwardly, it still means quite a bit to some, yet nothing at all to others, and therefore cannot be the basis of unity. What binds Canada together outside Quebec is thus no longer a common provenance, and less and less is it a common history. But people find the bonding elements in political institutions and ways of being. This is not a total break from the old identity, because Britishness also defined itself largely in terms of political institutions: parliamentary gov-ernment, a certain juridical tradition, and the like. The slide has been continuous and without a sharp break from the old to the new. There are even certain continuing elements, but the package is different.

Canadians feel that they are different from the Americans, because (a) they live in a less violent and conflict-ridden society. This is partly just a matter of luck. We do not have a history that has generated an undeclared, low-level race war continually feeding itself in our cities. It is also a matter of political culture. From the very beginning, Americans have put a value on ener-getic, direct defence of rights and therefore are ready to mitigate their condemnation of violence. There is more understanding of violence south of the border, more willingness to make allowances for it. This has something to do with the actual level of violence being higher there, as well as with a number of strange penchants of American society, such as that expressed in the powerful lobby for personal firearms. Canadians tend to put more value on "peace, order and good government." At least, this is how we see ourselves, which is perhaps what is important for our purposes; but there seems to be some truth in the perception.

As a consequence, there is more tolerance here of rules and restrictions that are justified by the need for order. With it, there is more of a favourable prejudice (at least in English Canada) and a free gift of the benefit of the doubt to the police forces. Hence the relative absence of protest when the War Measures Act was invoked in 1970; hence also the strange reluctance of the Canadian public to condemn the RCMP, even after all the revelations of its dubious behaviour. We might add that the Americans' tolerance of conflict extends into the domain of law as well. They are more litigious than we are. They think this is a good thing, that it reflects well on them. No one should take any guff from anyone. We tend to deplore it. From an American point of view, we seem to have an endless appetite for guff. But perhaps the long-term effect of the 1982 Charter of Rights and Freedoms will be to diminish this difference.

Related to this first point is a second point (b) that Canadians see their political society as more committed to collective provision, over against an American society that gives greater weight to individual initiative. Appeals for reduced government can be heard from the right of the political spectrum in both countries, but the idea of what reduced government actually means seems to be very different. There are regional differences in Canada, but generally Canadians are proud of and happy with their social programs, especially health insurance, and find the relative absence of these in the United States disturbing. The fact that poverty and destitution have been left to proliferate in American cities as they did during the Reagan years is generally seen here as a black mark against that society. Canadian practice may not be as much better as many of us believe, but the important point is that this is seen as a difference worth preserving.

Thus these two answers – (a) law and order, and (b) collective provision – help to address the distinctness question. They explain why we are a distinct political unit and why we want to remain so. But what answers the unity question? Why be a single country, and what common goals ought to animate this country? In one sense (a) and (b) can serve here as well if we think (as many Canadians instinctively do) that we need to hang together in order to maintain this alternative political culture as a viable option in North America. Moreover (b) can be logically extended into one of the principal declared common objectives of the Canadian federation in recent decades, namely (c) the equalization of life conditions and life chances between the regions. The solidarity of collective provision, which within each regional society generates such programs as Medicare, can be seen as finding its logical expression in a solidarity of mutual help between regions.

So Canadian federalism has generated the practices of large-scale redistribution of fiscal resources through equalization payments, and attempts have been made at regional development. This, too, contrasts with recent American practice and provides a further answer to the distinctness question. We perhaps owe the drive to equality to the fact that we have been confronted with existential questions in a way that our neighbours have not since 1865. The Canadian federal union has been induced to justify itself, and greater interregional solidarity may be one of the fruits of this underlying *angst*.

But this bonding principle has also been a worrying source of division, because it is widely seen as a locus of failed aspirations and disappointed expectations. The principles of regional equality and mutual help run against a perceived reality of central Canadian domination in the outlying regions, a grievous mismatch of promise and performance. Recently it has become clearer that the disappointment takes two rather different forms, reflecting different ideas of regional equality. In some parts, mainly Atlantic Canada, it is principally the failure of federal programs actually to improve regional economic standards that is the source of disappointment. The failure is one of mutual help. Elsewhere, mainly in western Canada, the sense of grievance is mobilized around neglected interests: the regions are not listened to, their interests are ridden over roughshod by a dominant central Canada. The failure is one of balance of power. In one version, the implicit but undelivered contract calls for redistribution to poorer regions. In the other version, it calls for a redress of power and influence in favour of the regions that have less demographic and economic clout. In one case, the implicit promise is of equalized incomes; in the other, it points to more equalized power between regional societies. It is clear that this issue of regional equality is a very troubled one in Canada. This is because it is on one hand an indispensable part of the answer to the unity question, while on the other it seems to many to be largely unrealized – and on top of it all, we agree less and less on what it actually means.

Even if things were going swimmingly in this domain, we still would not have a full answer to the unity question. Over the decades English Canada has been becoming more and more diverse and less an less "English." The fact that it has always been an immigrant society, (that is, one that functions through admitting a steady stream of new arrivals), on top of the fact that it could not aspire to make immigrants over to its original mould, has meant that it has de facto become more and more multicultural over the years. It could not aspire to assimilate the newcomers to an existing mould, because this mould was originally British, hence ethnic. In the United States, which has always operated on a strong sense that it incarnates unrivalled political institutions, the drive to make everyone American could proceed apace. It was never as clear what the Canadian identity amounted to in political terms, and insofar as it was conceived as British it could not be considered normative for new arrivals. First, it was only the identity of one part of the country and, second, it could not but come to be seen as one ethnic background among others.

Canadians have seen their society as less of a melting pot than the United States; and there has been some truth in this. In contrast to the neighbour society, people have spoken of a Canadian "mosaic." So this has even become, for some, a new facet of their answer to the distinctiveness question, under the rubric (d) multiculturalism. This is also far from trouble-free. Questions are being posed in both the major cultures about the pace and even goals of integration, or assimilation of immigrants into the larger anglophone or francophone society. This is particularly troubling in Quebec, which has much less historic experience of assimilating immigrants and a much higher proportion of whose francophone population is *pure laine.*

This makes even more acute the need for a further point of unity, a common reference point of identity, which can rally people from many diverse backgrounds and regions. In a quite astonishing way (e) the Charter of Rights and Freedoms has come to fill this role in English Canada in the past few years. It is astonishing, because as recently as 1980 it did not exist. Nor was there that much of a groundswell of support demanding its introduction before it became a bone of contention between federal and provincial governments in the run-up to the patriation of 1981–82. But the Meech Lake debate showed how important it has become in COQ, not just as an additional bulwark of rights but as part of the indispensable common ground on which all Canadians ought to stand. For many people, it has come in the space of a few years to define in part the Canadian political identity.[3] And since in COQ the national identity has to be defined in terms of political institutions (for reasons rehearsed above), this has been a fateful development.

WHY QUEBEC?

How about Quebec? How can it go about answering its existential question? The terms are very different. In Quebec, there is not a distinctness issue. The language and culture by themselves mark us off from Americans, and also from other Canadians. Much of (a) to (e) is seen as a "good thing" in Quebec. Regarding (a) – law and order – people do not compare themselves a lot with the United States, but there is no doubt that Quebeckers are spontaneously on the side of law and order and are even more horrified by internecine conflict than other Canadians are. The members of the FLQ utterly and totally relegated themselves to irrecoverable history as soon as they murdered Pierre Laporte. The rather half-hearted attempts to romanticize their escapades on the twentieth anniversary of the October Crisis in 1990 should not mislead in this regard. The reaction to the massacre of the women at Montreal's Ecole Polytechnique in 1989 is also eloquent on this score. Quebec society reacted more like a wounded family than like a large-scale, impersonal political unit.

Regarding (b) – collective provision – it goes without saying that people are proud of their social programs in the province and want to keep them. Point (d) – multiculturalism – is more problematic. As a federal policy, multiculturalism is sometimes seen as a device to deny French-speaking minorities their full recognition, or even to reduce the importance of the French fact in Canada to that of an outsized ethnic minority. Meanwhile, within Quebec itself, the growing diversity of francophone society is causing much heartburn and anxiety. Point (c) – regional equality and mutual self-help – is generally supported in Quebec, and even (e)

– the Charter – was viewed favourably until it came to be perceived as an instrument for the advancement of the uniformity of language regimes across the country. Even now its other provisions are widely popular.

But these do not go very far to answer the question "What is a country for?" There is one obvious answer to this question, which has continued down through the decades for over two centuries, namely (f) that one needs a country in order to defend or promote the nation. The nation here was originally *la nation canadienne-française*. Now, without entirely abandoning the first formulation, it tends to be put as *la nation québécoise*. This does not betoken any change in ethnic identity, of course. Rather, it reflects a sense, which presents itself as realistic but may be too pessimistic, that the really survivable elements of *la nation canadienne-française* are to be found only in Quebec. But the real point here is that (f) makes the survival and/or flourishing of this nation/language one of the prime goals of political society. No political entity is worth allegiance that does not contribute to this. The issue, independent Quebec versus remaining in Canada, turns simply on different judgments about what does contribute to this.

Put in terms of a possible formula for Canada, this means that from a Quebec perspective (a) to (e) may be attractive features, but the absolutely crucial one that Canada must have in order to possess a *raison d'être* is that it contribute to the survival and/or furtherance of *la nation canadienne-française*. This means in practice some kind of dualism. It was this, of course, that successive Quebec leaders always gave expression to when they described Canada as a pact between two nations, or two founding peoples.

Dualism in turn had to exist at two levels: (i) It meant that French had to be recognized as a language along with English in the federation; that is, French had to be given a status clearly different from that of an ethnic immigrant language, even if it was the most important among these; and (ii) it meant that *la nation canadienne-française*, or its major part, had to have some autonomy, some ability to act as a unit. Both these features were built to some degree into the original Confederation pact, but in the case of (i) – bilingualism – in partial and somewhat grudging form. Bilingualism (i) and Quebec autonomy (ii) are separate requirements, but they are also in a sense related. There is a certain degree of complementarity in that the more freely and completely (i) is granted, in theory the less the need will be felt for autonomous action. It is perhaps the tragedy of Canada that (i) was eventually granted too late and too grudgingly, and that this established a high and irreversible pattern of demands on (ii).

Both these requirements have been a source of difficulty. The extension of (i) beyond its original limits raised a problem, because COQ in its developing multiculturalism was naturally led to accord English the status of a common language and to split language from culture. That English was the main language was not meant to imply that people of English descent had privileges or were somehow superior. The hegemony of English had to be justified in purely utilitarian terms. Within this framework, the case for putting French alongside English was impossible to make. Outside Quebec, a special status for French was rarely justified by numbers, and certainly not by its indispensability as a medium of communication. It seemed like indefensible favouritism. Secondly, both (i) and (ii) met with resistance because of a perceived difference of Quebec from the values of the rest of Canada. This started off as a dark prejudice in the mind of Orange Protestants, but it has continued on in many another milieux because of the supposed appeal of illiberal modes of thought in Quebec. In particular, this militated against further concessions in the area of (ii).

It has been one of the remarkable achievements of the last thirty years, and particularly of the Trudeau government, to have established bilingualism (i) almost integrally. There has been a certain cost in resentment in some areas, and this may be fateful in forthcoming negotiations. I want to return to this below. But there is no doubt that a big change has been brought about. On Quebec autonomy (ii) as well, great progress has been made. First, the Canadian federation has proven a very flexible instrument, giving lots of powers to the provinces. And second, where Quebec's needs have been different from the other provinces, a large de facto special status has been developed. Quebec has its own pension plan, levies its own income tax, has a special immigration regime, and so on.

But it is the formal recognition of Quebec's autonomy that has been blocked. Giving Quebec the autonomy it needs, without disbalancing the Canadian federation, would involve giving

Quebec a different kind of relation to the federal government and institutions. Although this has been worked de facto to a remarkable extent, there is powerful resistance to according it recognition in principle. This is because there is a deep clash of purpose between the two sides of Canada. Where the old clash of values seems to have disappeared, a new conflict of purposes – of answers to the question "What is a country for?" – has surfaced.

The demands of (ii), of a special status for Quebec, run against those of regional equality (c) as these are conceived by many in coq, and against a widespread understanding of the Charter (e). Point (c) has come to be defined for some as entailing an equality of the provinces. The great moral force of the principle of equity between regions has been mobilized behind the rather abstract juridical issue of the relative constitutional status of provinces. Regional equity seems to be flouted if all provinces are not placed on the same footing. A special status can be presented as a breach in this kind of equality. More grievously, the special status for Quebec is plainly justified on the grounds of the defence and promotion of *la nation canadienne-française* (f). But this is a collective goal. The aim is to ensure the flourishing and survival of a community. The new patriotism of the Charter has given an impetus to a philosophy of rights and of non-discrimination that is highly suspicious of collective goals. It can only countenance them if they are clearly subordinated to individual rights and to provisions of non-discrimination. But for those who take these goals seriously, this subordination is unacceptable. The Charter and the promotion of the nation, as understood in their respective constituencies, are on a collision course. The reactions to Bill 178 and much of the Meech Lake debate were eloquent on this score.

This difficulty arises with the concept of Quebec autonomy (ii), where it did not for bilingualism (i). The provisions for bilingualism in federal legislation can be justified in terms of individual rights. They concern the guarantee that francophones can be dealt with and obtain government services in their own language. Once French is given this status along with English, what is protected are the rights of individuals. The collective goal goes beyond this. The aim is not only that francophones be served in French but that there still be francophones there in the next generation; this is the objective of (f). It cannot be translated into an assurance of rights for existing francophones. Indeed, pursuing it may even involve reducing their individual freedom of choice, as Bill 101 does in Quebec, where francophone parents must send their children to French-language schools.

So the two halves of Canada have come onto a collision course because of the conflict between their respective answers to the question "What is a country for?" – in particular, a conflict between regional equality and the Charter, on one hand, and Quebec autonomy, on the other. Other difficulties have been raised about special status – in particular, the problem of participation of Quebeckers in a federal parliament if the matters it deals with for other Canadians come to diverge greatly from the matters it deals with affecting Quebec. But I think this difficulty is exaggerated. The two areas of concern have to come very far apart for this to be a real problem.[4]

WHY NOW?

One might ask, why is the collision course occurring now? Surely the old "English" Canada, before the legislation about bilingualism and the Trudeau revolution, was even more inhospitable to the demands of Quebec. It baulked not only at Quebec autonomy but at bilingualism as well. Moreover, it penetrated much more within Quebec. In those days, the English minority, often backed by the federal government or pan-Canadian institutions such as the CPR, maintained its own English-only forms of operation, excluding or marginalizing or downgrading the French language. Why did things not fly apart then?

The answer is that separation did not seem a realistic option back then for all sorts of reasons. It started with a clear-sighted appreciation of the relation of forces and a sense of what the English-Canadian majority would tolerate. There was also a greater commitment to the francophone minorities outside the province than there now is. But an extremely important factor was the restricted economic role of French Quebeckers. The English still had a preponderant role in the economy. Big business spoke English; anglophones dominated the ranks of management and had more than their share of certain key economic professions such as engineering. This was a source of grievance on many levels. In particular, it was what permitted English to arrogate to itself a place in the province that demographics would never justify. To take just one instance, before the Quiet Revolution, again and again, union leaders would have to bargain in English with management on behalf of a work force that was 100 per cent francophone. But at the same time, this imbalance contributed to a climate in which Quebec society felt incomplete, in which essential functions were being filled by outsiders. The relation was never articulated in this way at the time, but it helped to keep the option of a total break off the agenda. Separation was not a real option before 1960, even though it seems to have been toyed with by Abbé Groulx as an eventual long-term destination.

Paradoxically, as some of the most crying grievances were resolved, as the insulting and sometimes threatening marginalization of the French language was reversed, as francophone Quebeckers began to take their full place in the economy – at first through the public and parapublic sectors (for example, Hydro-Québec) and then through the private sector – precisely in the wake of all these successes, the demand for independence gained strength. It grew until it became one of two major constitutional options, on a par with its federalist rival – and, since Meech Lake, even ahead of it. All this was going on while outside Quebec, at the federal level, bilingualism was advancing and Quebeckers were wielding more power than ever before. These are the years of "French power." Some westerners have the feeling that the federal government is run by Quebeckers. Why does breakup loom now? How can we explain this paradoxical and even perverse result?

Part of the answer, implicit in the above, is that now for the first time the option looks conceivable, possible, even safe. In this regard, even the last decade has seen a change. In 1980, most Quebeckers still found sovereignty a somewhat frightening prospect. The referendum revealed that clearly. In 1990, this no longer seems to be so. A great deal of the difference seems to stem from the currently perceived high-profile place of francophones as big players in our economic life. This is something that has been happening over a number of decades, but as is the way with media-driven public perceptions, the realization has come all in a rush. And with this realization has come a great flush of confidence. As so often with these media-driven perceptions, we go easily from one exaggeration to another. Quebeckers were not as powerless before and are not as powerful now as they think. Separation risks being much more economically costly than they now believe, even as it would have been less catastrophic than many thought in 1980. We may even be in for another swerve of opinion as the present recession dims expectations. But the basic change is undeniable. Separation is really thinkable.

Yet this cannot be the whole explanation. To claim so would be to say that Quebeckers never really wanted anything else, that they were just waiting for the moment when they could dare to go for it. And nothing could be falser than that. A great deal has attached francophone Quebeckers to this country: first of all, the sense that the larger entity was the home of *la nation canadienne-française,* whose whole extent included more than Quebec; then a certain attachment to a constitutional home which had become familiar and which their leaders had had a hand in building. But what was always missing was a genuine patriotism for Canada. That kind of sentiment was reserved for *la nation canadienne-française.* It has lately been transposed onto Quebec, as the viable segment of that nation, but has never managed to spread from there onto the whole political unit. This is why people have often spoken of Canada as being, for Quebeckers, a *mariage de raison* – a marriage of convenience. This somewhat understates the case, because it does not take account of the multiform attachment to Canada which I have just described, but it is emotionally true in this negative sense that a genuine patriotism for a bilingual, two-nation Canada has never developed among Quebeckers. This by itself still does not explain the strength of the independentist option today. After all, if Canada is a *mariage de raison,* why abandon it when it has never been so reasonable and when the deal seems the most favourable ever? Of course, many federalist Quebeckers are pleading the cause of Canada today in just these terms. But why does it not have more success? Why are even those who are making the plea profoundly ambivalent about it?

Here one can easily be misled, because the opponents of these partisans of "profitable federalism" seem to want to engage them on their own ground and strive to prove that Confederation is a bad deal for us. But, in fact, the emotional drive behind independence is elsewhere. It is much more a failure of recognition.

For decades, Quebec leaders explained that Confederation was a pact between two founding peoples, two nations. This was never the way the matter was understood outside the province. But the claim was not so much to the effect that this was the plain sense of the confederation pact, somehow perversely forgotten by the others – although this is how it was often put. It was much more an expression of the profound sentiment that this was the only form in which Confederation could ultimately be acceptable to French Canadians in a way that could engage their hearts and respect their dignity.

In fact, in the real world it was necessary to live with compromises, in which the duality principle got a rather limited and grudging expression. It was necessary to operate in a country which for many purposes was run much more as a nation with one hegemonic culture, with more or less generous provision for minorities on a regional basis. Present-day Canadians, some of whom still may want to complain about the number of languages on their cornflakes boxes, have no idea of how exiguous the place of French was in the bad old days. In the 1930s even the money was still unilingually English.

Canada had to be accepted, but never so as to engage the heart or respect dignity. It could not be accepted *dans l'honneur et l'enthousiasme*, to use a phrase that was so often repeated during the drama of Meech Lake. Below the rational acceptance of the marriage of convenience, these denials bite deep. This is easy to lose sight of, because those who are frustrated in their desire for recognition understandably do not want to present their case in those terms. It is only when one is recognized that one is happy to avow the desire. So the phrase *dans l'honneur et l'enthousiasme* emerged when it looked as though the aspiration was at last met. But when it is denied, the opponents of federal Canada will pretend that no one was ever interested in mere symbols, that the calculus of independence is made in the realistic terms of power and prosperity, that the attitudes of the English-Canadian partner mean nothing to us. In all this, they do protest a little too much.

The present strength of independentism is thus due in part to the new confidence of Quebeckers and in part to the fact that Canada has never gelled as a nation for them. But in large part it is also due to the continued denial of their understanding of

Canada, of the only terms on which it could have been fully accepted by them. These were articulated, among other forms, in the "two nations" view of the country. Of course, this was unacceptable to the rest of the country, which did not itself feel like a "nation." Here there was an attempt by French Canadians to foist a symmetrical identity on their partners. And this attempt has not yet been abandoned, as one can see from much of the discussion in Quebec today, to which I will return below. But there was a basic demand that could be separated from this presumptuous definition of the other. This was the demand that *la nation canadienne-française* be recognized as a crucial component of the country, as an entity whose survival and flourishing was one of the main purposes of Canada as a political society. If this had been granted, it would not have mattered how the rest of the country defined itself.

Actually, the country has come to arrange itself not at all badly for this purpose, through federal bilingualism, through advances made by some French-speaking minorities elsewhere, and through a de facto administrative special status for Quebec. But what was missing was a clear recognition that this was part of our purpose as a federation. This is why Meech Lake was so important and why its failure will have such dire consequences. If one just listens to what people say in Quebec, this can seem strange. Lots of Quebeckers never even admitted that they were in favour of Meech, or expressed lukewarm support. Basically, all the independentists took this line. Those who were sceptical about English Canada hedged their bets, never wanting to allow that the recognition mattered to them. But the depth of the reaction to its demise shows how little this represented how they felt.

The Meech Lake Accord was important because it was the first time that recognition of Canadian duality and the special role of Quebec was being written into a statement of what Canada was about. The fact that the accord conferred no additional powers largely narrowed its significance to this one clear declaration of intent. The importance of this declaration can be understood only in the light of the years of non-recognition, of the marriage of convenience that failed to engage the heart and reflect dignity. It can be understood in the context of a present generation that is free of the timidity of its ancestors in facing a possible break and is even a little surprised, sometimes a trifle contemptuous of its predecessors for having put up with non-recognition for so long. Thus, the rejection of the accord, when it was just this, purely a declaration of intent, takes on fateful significance. (This is the point of the oft-repeated phrase that Meech constituted our minimal conditions).

With the demise of Meech, something snapped. I think it can be rather simply described. Quebeckers would no longer live in a structure that did not fully recognize their national goals. In the early 1980s, after the defeat of the "yes" in the referendum, many toyed with the idea of accepting the marriage of convenience, and making a go of it with or without recognition. The new confidence could also have been motivated by this rather different stance, which marginalized the issue of recognition. After all, if you know your own worth, why do you need the other? But, in a sense, Meech wiped out this possibility just because it raised the hope of recognition.

What remains to be explained is the extraordinary euphoria that all observers noted among the crowds celebrating Quebec's national holiday, the Saint-Jean 1990. Why did Quebeckers feel so united and so relieved at being united – almost as though the demise of Meech had taken a great weight off them? I think it was because the long division and hesitation between the "reasonable" acceptance of a structure that did not recognize them and the insistence on having their national purposes openly accepted had at last been resolved. This was felt as a division between Quebeckers and was especially painful at the time of the 1980 referendum when families were often split. But it also divided many Quebeckers within themselves. At last the long conflict, the long hesitation, the long ambivalence was over. Quebeckers were clear about what they wanted to ask of any future political structure on the northern half of this continent. Consensus was recovered, but also a kind of psychic unity. It seemed that a certain kind of compromise was over forever.

But what did this mean for the future? It meant that demand (ii) for Quebec autonomy had become imperious and virtually nonnegotiable. And this brought a real danger of breach between the two parts of the country. For it followed that Quebeckers would not accept any structure in which their collective aspirations were

out the silliness, contempt, and ill will, there remains a serious point here. Indeed, there are two kinds of serious points. First, there is a genuine difference in philosophy concerning the bases of a liberal society. Second, there is a difference in view about the basis for national unity.

Let us take the philosophical difference first. Those who take the view that individual rights must always come first and, along with non-discrimination provisions, must take precedence over collective goals, are often speaking out of a view of a liberal society that has become more and more widespread in the Anglo-American world. Its source is, of course, the United States, and it has recently been elaborated and defended by some of the best philosophical and legal minds in that society, for instance John Rawls, Ronald Dworkin, Bruce Ackerman, and others.[6] There are various formulations of the main idea, but perhaps the one that encapsulates most clearly the point that is relevant to us is Dworkin's way of putting things in his short paper entitled "Liberalism."[7]

Dworkin makes a distinction between two kinds of moral commitment. We all have views about the ends of life, about what constitutes a good life that we and others ought to strive for; but we also acknowledge a commitment to deal fairly and equally with one another, regardless of how we conceive our ends. We might call the latter "procedural" commitments, while those that concern the ends of life are "substantive." Dworkin claims that a liberal society is one which, as a society, adopts no particular substantive view about the ends of life. Rather, the society is united around strong procedural commitments to treat people with equal respect. The reason why the polity as such can espouse no substantive view – why it cannot, for instance, allow that one of the goals of legislation should be to make people virtuous in one or the other meaning of that term – is that this would involve a violation of its procedural norm; for, granted the diversity of modern societies, it would unfailingly be the case that some people and not others would be committed to the favoured conception of virtue. They might be in a majority; indeed, it is very likely that they would be, for otherwise a democratic society would probably not espouse their view. Nevertheless, this view would not be everyone's, and in espousing this substantive outlook the society would not be treating the dissident minority with equal respect. In effect, it would be saying to them, "Your view is not as valuable, in the eyes of this polity, as the view of your more numerous compatriots."

There are very profound philosophical assumptions underlying this view of liberalism, which is influenced by the thought of the late-eighteenth-century German philosopher, Immanuel Kant. Among other features, this view understands human dignity to consist largely in autonomy – in the ability of each person to determine for him or herself a view of the good life. That is, dignity is connected less with any particular understanding of the good life, such that someone's departure from this would be a derogation from his or her own dignity, than it is with the power to consider and espouse for oneself some view or other. We are not respecting this power equally in all subjects, it is claimed, if we officially raise the outcome of some people's deliberations over that of others. A liberal society must remain neutral on the good life and must restrict itself to ensuring that however citizens see things, they deal fairly with one another and that the state deals equally with all.

The popularity of this view of the human agent as primarily a subject of self-determining or self-expressive choice helps to explain why this model of liberalism is so strong. There is also the fact that it has been urged with great force and intelligence by liberal thinkers in the United States, and precisely in the context of constitutional doctrines of judicial review.[8] So it is not surprising that the idea becomes accredited, well beyond those who might subscribe to a specific Kant-derived philosophy, that a liberal society cannot accommodate publicly espoused notions of the good. This is the conception, as Michael Sandel has called it, of the "procedural republic,"[9] which has a very strong hold on the political agenda in the United States and which has helped to place increasing emphasis on judicial review on the basis of constitutional texts at the expense of the ordinary political process of building majorities with a view to legislative action.

But a society with collective goals like Quebec's violates this model. It is axiomatic for Quebec governments that the survival and flourishing of French culture in Quebec is a good. Political society is not neutral between those who value remaining true to the culture of our ancestors and those who might want to cut loose in the name of some individual goal of self-development. It might be argued that one could after all capture a goal like *survivance* for a proceduralist liberal society. One could consider the French language, for instance, as a collective resource that individuals might want to make use of, and act for its preservation, just as one does for clean air or green spaces. But this cannot capture the full thrust of policies designed for cultural survival. It is not just a matter of having the French language available for those who might choose it (which might be seen to have been the goal of some of the measures of federal bilingualism over the last twenty years). It is also a matter of making sure that there is a community of people here in the future that will want to avail itself of this opportunity. Policies aimed at survival actively seek to create members of the community – for instance, in assuring that the rising generations go on identifying as French speakers, or whatever. There is no way that they could be seen as just providing a facility to already existing people.[10]

Quebeckers therefore, and those who give similar importance to this kind of collective goal, tend to opt for a rather different model of a liberal society. On this view, a society can be organized around a definition of the good life, without this being seen as a depreciation of those who do not personally share this definition. Where the nature of the good requires that it be sought in common, this is the reason for its being an object of public policy. According to this conception, a liberal society singles itself out as such by the way in which it treats minorities, including those who do not share public definitions of the good; and, above all, by the rights it accords to all its members. In this case, the rights in question are conceived to be the fundamental and crucial ones that have been recognized as such from the very beginning of the liberal tradition: the right to life, liberty, due process, free speech, free practise of religion, and the like. On this model, there is something exaggerated, a dangerous overlooking of an essential boundary, in speaking of fundamental rights to such things as commercial signage in the language of one's choice. One has to distinguish between, on the one hand, the fundamental liberties – those which should never at any time be infringed and which therefore ought to be unassailably entrenched – and, on the other hand, the privileges and immunities which are important but can be revoked or restricted for reasons of public policy (although one needs a strong reason to do so).

A society with strong collective goals can be liberal, on this view, provided it is also capable of respecting diversity, especially when this concerns those who do not share its goals, and provided it can offer adequate safeguards for fundamental rights. There will undoubtedly be tensions involved, and difficulties, in pursuing these objectives together, but they are not uncombinable, and the problems are not in principle greater than those encountered by any liberal society that has to combine liberty and equality, for example, or prosperity and justice.

Here are two incompatible views of liberal society. One of the great sources of our recent disunity has been that they have come to square off against each other in the last decade. The resistance to the distinct society which called for precedence to be given to the Charter came in part from a spreading procedural outlook in English Canada. From this point of view, attributing the goal of promoting Quebec's distinct society to a government was to acknowledge a collective goal, and this move had to be neutralized by being subordinated to the existing Charter. From the standpoint of Quebec, this attempt to impose a procedural model of liberalism not only would deprive the "distinct society" clause of some of its force as a rule of interpretation, but it bespoke a rejection of the model of liberalism on which this society had come to be founded. There was a lot of misperception by each society of the other throughout the Meech Lake debate, as I mentioned above. But here both saw something right about the other – and did not like it. coq saw that the "distinct society" clause legitimated collective goals. And Quebec saw that the move to give the Charter precedence imposed a form of liberal society that was alien and to which Quebec could never accommodate itself without surrendering its identity. In this context, the protestations by Charter patriots that they were not "against Quebec" rang hollow.

This was one source of deep disagreement. There was also a second one, which was interwoven with it. The Charter has taken on tremendous importance in coq not only because of the growing force of procedural liberalism but also because, in the steadily increasing diversity of this multicultural society, people are looking for new bases of unity. COQ has also seen its reason for existence partly in terms of its political institutions, for reasons discussed above. Even though the Charter offers a relatively weak answer to the distinctness question, because it makes us more like the United States, it nevertheless can provide a convincing answer to the unity question. The two motives for Charter patriotism come together here. As the country gets more diverse, we are more and more acutely aware of the divergences in our conceptions of the good life. It then appears that what can and ought to bind us together are precisely the procedural norms that govern our interaction. Procedural liberalism not only begins to look more plausible in itself, but it also seems to be the only unquestionable common ground.

But if the Charter is really serving as common ground, it is hard to accept that its meaning and application may be modulated in one part of the country, by something like the "distinct society" clause, differently from the way it applies in others. The resistance to this clause of the Meech Lake Accord came partly from the sense that the Charter of all things had to apply in the same way to all Canadians. If the procedural bond is the only thing that can hold us together without ranking some above others, then it has to hold without exception.

Can this conflict be arbitrated? In a sense, no. One side insists on holding the country together around a model of liberalism which the other cannot accept. If there is to be agreement, this first side has to give way. But in another sense, the possible common ground is obvious. Procedural liberals in English Canada just have to acknowledge, first, that there are other possible models of liberal society and, second, that their francophone compatriots wish to live by one such alternative. That the first is true becomes pretty evident once one looks around at the full gamut of contemporary free societies in Europe and elsewhere, instead of attending only to the United States. The truth of the second should be clear to anyone with a modicum of knowledge of Quebec history and politics.

But once you accept both, it is clear that the attempt to make procedural liberalism the basis of Canadian unity is both illegitimate and doomed to failure. For it represents an imposition of one society's model on another, and in the circumstances of late-twentieth century Canadian democracy this cannot succeed. The only way we can coexist is by allowing ourselves to differ on this. Does this mean that we can only coexist as two independent societies, perhaps loosely linked by supranational institutions? This is the thesis of Quebec sovereigntists. But this has never seemed to me to be self-evident. It becomes true only to the extent that procedural liberals stand so firmly on principle that they cannot stand sharing the same country with people who live by another model. Rigidity of this kind began to be evident during the Meech Lake debate. If this were to be COQ's last word, then indeed the independentists are right and there is no solution short of sovereignty association.

EQUALITY OF WHAT?

The second great area of conflict is between the demands of a special status for Quebec and those of regional equality, once this is interpreted as requiring equality between the provinces. But whereas over the two models of liberalism there is really a genuine philosophic difference underlying all the misunderstanding, here there is still much mutual misperception and cross purposes. For, in fact, the two demands come out of quite different agendas, as has often been remarked. The demand for special status is usually one for assuming a wider range of responsibilities and hence for greater autonomy. The call for regional equality comes generally from those who feel that their interests have been given insufficient weight in federal policy making, and hence aim for more clout in this process. One side wants to take a greater distance form the central government and legislature. The other wants a weightier place within them. That is why it has taken the form in recent years of a call for reform in federal institutions, notably the Senate.

So understood, these demands are not logically opposed. Of course, they can at many points get in each other's way. There has been a fear among provinces that look to a more active federal government to equalize conditions across the regions, that excessive powers to Quebec might end up weakening the power of the centre to act. This may indeed occur, but it is not fated to do so. It is not the reflection of a logical conflict, such as that between equality of all provinces, on the one hand, and special powers for one of them, on the other. The demands for special status and strong central government can possibly be made compatible. What has made this difficult in practice has been precisely the refusal to depart from uniformity. This has meant that any "concession" to Quebec has had to be offered to all the provinces. Fortunately, these have not always been taken up, and so we have evolved quite a considerable de facto special status for Quebec, as I remarked above. But it has never been possible to proceed in that direction openly and explicitly, because of the pressure for uniformity. In the Meech Lake Accord itself, which was designed to address the difficulties of Quebec, most of what was accorded to Quebec had to be distributed to all the others.

The language of "equality" between provinces has in fact been a source of confusion, screening the reality of what is at stake and making solution more difficult. Equality is a notoriously difficult concept to apply and depends on the respect one makes salient. It could be argued that Quebec needs powers that other provinces do not, to cope with problems and a vocation that other provinces do not have. Accordingly, this point could be seen as a move towards equality (to each province according to its tasks), not away from it. Moreover, the special status has nothing to do with having more clout at the centre. It involves something quite different.

All of this should encourage us to think that it may not be beyond human wit to discover a way to satisfy these different demands together. There are (a) provinces which want more say in the decisions of the federal government. There are others which, while not disinterested in this first goal, are mainly concerned with (b) maintaining an active federal government as a force for economic and social equalization between regions. Then there is Quebec, which (c) wants the powers it thinks essential to the preservation and promotion of its distinct society. To this we now have to add the aboriginal dimension. This means that our arrangements have to accommodate the need for forms of self-government and self-management appropriate to the different First Nations. This may mean in practice allowing for a new form of jurisdiction in Canada, perhaps weaker than the provinces, but, unlike municipalities, not simply the creatures of another level of government.

Putting all this together will be very difficult. It will take much ingenuity and good will – perhaps more of either than we possess. But the task will be utterly impossible if we persist in describing the problem in the misleading and often demagogic language of equality versus inequality of provinces. Put in these terms, the problem is a false one, and the present importance of this formulation is a sign of our lack of lucidity and the decline of good will. It reflects the deep mutual suspicions that have come to cloud our political scene.

The game of multidimensional constitutional tug-of-war that we have been playing in Canada these past years has made our situation worse, partly by creating or strengthening unhealthy linkages, whereby aspirations that are, as such, perfectly compatible come to be seen as deadly rivals. Examples are the linkages made between linguistic duality and multiculturalism, or those between aboriginals and Québécois, or those between regional equality and the distinct society. It may already be too late to climb out of the skein of resentments and mutual suspicion, and it will take far-sighted and courageous leadership to do so. But it will also require that we see each other's aspirations for what they are, as free as possible from the rhetoric of resentment.

LEVELS OF DIVERSITY

Various solutions can be glimpsed beyond the present stalemate. One set would be based on a dualism in which Quebec would no longer be a federal unit just like the others. The other possible range would have as its basis a four- or five-region federalism that was decentralized enough to accommodate Quebec as a member on all fours with the rest. Either type of solution would have to accommodate difference in a way we have not yet succeeded in doing – at least openly and admittedly. Can we do it? It looks bad, but I would like to close by saying a few words about what this might mean.

In a way, accommodating difference is what Canada is all about. Many Canadians would concur in this. That is why the mutual suspicion and ill will that has so often accompanied the constitutional debate has been so painful to many of our compatriots. It is not just that the two sources of difference I have been describing are becoming more salient. Old questions may be reopened. To some extent, Trudeau's remarkable achievement in extending bilingualism was made possible by a growing sympathy towards the French fact among political and social élites in COQ. The élites pushed the bilingual process at a pace faster than many of their fellow citizens wanted. For many people lower down in the hierarchy, French was being "stuffed down their throats," but because of the élite-run nature of the political accommodation process in this country, they seemed to have no option but to take it.

During the Meech debate the procedures of élite negotiation came under sharp criticism and challenge. Moreover, the COQ élites were themselves split on how to respond to the new package, in a way they had not been on bilingualism. It was therefore not surprising that we began to see a rebellion against the accommodation of French. This might be the harbinger of greater resistance to come. Already one hears westerners saying that Canadian duality is an irrelevancy to them, that their experience of Canada is of a multicultural mosaic. The very bases of a two-language federation are being questioned again. This important axis of difference is under threat.

More fundamentally, we face a challenge to our very conception of diversity. Many of the people who rallied around the Charter and multiculturalism to reject the distinct society are proud of their acceptance of diversity – and in some respects rightly so. What is enshrined here is what one might call first-level diversity. There are great differences in culture and outlook and background in a population that nevertheless shares the same idea of what it is to belong to Canada. Their patriotism or manner of belonging is uniform, whatever their other differences, and this is felt to be a necessity if the country is to hold together.

This is far from accommodating all Canadians. For Quebeckers, and for most French Canadians, the way of being a Canadian (for those who still want to be) is by their belonging to a constituent element of Canada, *la nation québécoise*, or *canadienne-française*. Something analogous holds for aboriginal communities in this country; their way of being Canadian is not accommodated by first-level diversity. Yet many people in COQ are puzzled by the resulting sense of exclusion, because first-level diversity is the only kind to which they are sensitive and which they feel they fully acknowledge.

To build a country for everyone, Canada would have to allow for second-level or "deep" diversity, in which a plurality of ways of belonging would also be acknowledged and accepted. Someone of, say, Italian extraction in Toronto or Ukrainian extraction in Edmonton might indeed feel Canadian as a bearer of individual rights in a multicultural mosaic. His or her belonging would not "pass through" some other community, although the ethnic identity might be important to him or her in various ways. But this person might nevertheless accept that a Québécois or a Cree or a Déné might belong in a very different way, that these persons were Canadian through being members of their national communities. Reciprocally, the Québécois, Cree, or Déné would accept the perfect legitimacy of the "mosaic" identity.

Is this utopian? Could people ever come to see their country this way? Could they even find it exciting and an object of pride that they belong to a country that allows deep diversity? Pessimists say no, because they do not see how such a country could have a sense of unity. The model of citizenship has to be uniform, or people would have no sense of belonging to the same polity. Those who say so tend to take the United States as their paradigm, which has indeed been hostile to deep diversity and has sometimes tried to stamp it out as "un-American."

These pessimists should bear in mind three things. First, deep diversity is the only formula on which a united federal Canada can be rebuilt, once we recall the reasons why we all need Canada – namely, for law and order, collective provision, regional equality, and mutual self-help, as mentioned above. Second, in many parts of the world today the degree and nature of the differences resemble those of Canada rather than the United States. If a uniform model of citizenship fits better the classical image of the Western liberal state, it is also true that this is a straightjacket for many political societies. The world needs other models to be legitimated in order to allow for more humane and less constraining modes of political cohabitation. Instead of pushing ourselves to the point of breakup in the name of the uniform model, we would do our own and some other peoples a favour by exploring the space of deep diversity. To those who believe in according people the freedom to be themselves, this would be counted a gain in civilization. In this exploration we would not be alone. Europe watchers have noticed how the development of the European Community has gone along with an increased breathing space for regional societies – Breton, Basque, Catalan – which were formerly threatened with the steamroller of the national state.

Finally, after dividing to form two polities with uniform citizenship, both of the successor states would find that they had failed after all to banish the challenge of deep diversity; because the only way that they can do justice to their aboriginal populations is by adopting a pluralist mould. Neither Quebec nor coq could succeed in imitating the United States – or the European national states in their chauvinist prime. So let us recognize this now and take the road of deep diversity together.

Notes

1 "La Province de Québec au moment de la grève," in *La Grève de l'amiante*, ed. Pierre Trudeau (Montréal: les Éditions Cité Libre, 1956).
2 In Quebec we speak blithely of "English Canada," but the people who live there do not identify with this label. We need a handy way of referring to the rest of the country as an entity, even if it lacks for the moment political expression. In order to avoid the clumsy "Canada outside Quebec," I plan to use "coq" henceforth in this chapter. I hope the reader will not take this as a sign of encroaching barbarism or of Québécois self-absorption (although it might partake in no small measure of both).
3 Alan Cairns has written very insightfully on this development. See in particular his "Constitutional Minoritarianism in Canada," in *Canada: The State of the Federation 1990*, ed. Ronald L. Watts and Douglas M. Brown (Kingston: Institute of Intergovernmental Relations, Queen's University, 1990); and "Ritual, Taboo and Bias in Constitutional Controversies in Canada, or Constitutional Talk Canadian Style," in *The Saskatchewan Law Review* 54 (1990): 121–47.
4 I do not wish to dwell on this point at length here, but our own experience and that of some other countries seem to reduce our grounds for worry on this score. We have to remember that Quebec already has a special status. In 1964, Quebec members sat in the House of Commons while the Canada Pension Plan was voted,

following an agreement with Quebec that the province would have its own plan. The fact that there was a separate Quebec plan did not mean that Quebeckers had no further interest in the Canadian arrangements. On the contrary, because of the demands of portability, each was vitally interested in the other. Other examples of asymmetrical relations between a part and the whole include the "provincial" government that existed for many years in Ulster. This experiment was terminated for reasons that had nothing to do with any constitutional unworkability.

5 For instance, the First Amendment, which forbade Congress from establishing any religion, was not originally meant to separate state and church as such. It was enacted at a time when many states had established churches, and it was plainly meant to prevent the new federal government from interfering with or overruling these local arrangements. It was only later after the Fourteenth Amendment, following the so-called incorporation doctrine, that these restrictions on the federal government were held to have been extended to all governments at whatever level.

6 John Rawls, *A Theory of Justice* (Cambridge, Mass.: Harvard University Press, 1971), and "Justice as Fairness: Political not Metaphysical," *Philosophy and Public Affairs* 14 (1985): 223–57; Ronald Dworkin, *Taking Rights Seriously* (London: Duckworth, 1977), and "Liberalism," in *Public and Private Morality*, ed. Stuart Hampshire (Cambridge: Cambridge University Press, 1978); Bruce Ackerman, *Social Justice in the Liberal State* (New Haven: Yale University Press, 1980).

7 Dworkin, "Liberalism."

8 See, for instance, the arguments deployed by Lawrence Tribe in his *Abortion: The Clash of Absolutes* (New York: Norton, 1990).

9 Michael Sandel, "The Procedural Republic and the Unencumbered Self," *Political Theory* 12 (February 1984): 81–96.

10 An ingenious argument has recently been put forward by Will Kymlicka in his brilliant book, *Liberalism, Community and Culture* (Oxford: Clarendon Press, 1989). He argues that what I have been calling procedural liberalism can be made compatible with the defence of collective rights and cultural survival in certain cases. Kymlicka, unlike the major American authors, writes in full knowledge of the Canadian scene and with a strong commitment to the defence of aboriginal rights in this country. While espousing a politics of "neutral moral concern" – that is, a view of the liberal state as neutral between

conceptions of the good life (76) – he nevertheless argues that collective cultural rights can be defended on the grounds that the members of certain threatened communities would be deprived of the conditions of intelligent, self-generated decisions about the good life if the "cultural structures" through which they can grasp the options are undermined (165). If Kymlicka's argument really prevailed, it would close the gap between the two models of liberalism that I am contrasting in these pages.

CHAPTER NINE

Impediments to a Canadian Future

Charles Taylor wrote this text in the spring of 1992 as uncertainty continued to gather on the political-constitutional horizon. He believes that the pursuit of recognition, which represents an important aspect of modern identity, is at the heart of the Canadian crisis. On this question, Taylor the citizen of Quebec and Canada meets Taylor the lucid analyst of Western civilization. Note that he had already touched on this theme in 1979, during a conference of the Canadian Philosophical Association (see chapter 3).

YEARS AGO, WHEN I WAS IN ISRAEL, I HEARD A JOKE that has remained with me ever since. It goes like this. An Israeli asks, "How did we ever end up in this terrible geographical situation, with enemies on every side?"

Answer: "It's all because Moses had a speech impediment."

"How so?"

"Well, when God had led the people of Israel out of Egypt, he asked Moses where they wanted to go. Where else but Canada. So Moses tried to tell God: 'Cana... Cana...' – till God lost patience and jumped to his own conclusions. 'O.K. I'll take you to Canaan,' he said. The rest is history."

I think of this every time I try to explain to someone from outside why our country is on the verge of breaking up. They can't understand. "You have everything – prosperity, peace, security – you are the envy of the world. Why are you throwing it away?" My problem is that as I try to communicate our situation to them,

I come more and more to see it from their point of view, and my own country seems weirder and weirder to me. So I want to have another try here, this time addressing my compatriots, which means that I can't cut any corners. But at least my readers will be inside the madness and not outside trying to peer in.

Why are we under threat of breakup? Part of the answer lies in that very peace and prosperity. We are so used to it that we have trouble imagining real adversity, the kind other countries live with all the time. But this is only part of the story. The root cause of our impending fracture can be put in one word: recognition. All people want to be recognized for what they are, but this need takes on a peculiar importance in modern society, where our sense of identity – what we want to be recognized as – is being defined in new and often original terms. I have tried to describe this general phenomenon elsewhere.[1] Here I want to concentrate on one aspect of it, that which affects not so much individuals but communities.

Mutual recognition between groups has come to be a crucial issue in modern politics because of the very nature of modern society. Liberal democracies operate on a common understanding – some would want to say "myth" – that they are ultimately ruled by the people. To be a member of a sovereign people is to be one of equal and autonomous citizens. If one is unequal, or is dependent on another, then one's own voice does not count, or is weighed at a discount, in the decisions of this sovereign entity. If a large number of members are dependent or unequal in this way, it is no longer true to say that the people are the sovereign body, for this applies only to the subsection that is independent and dominant. So it is crucial, if liberal democracy is to live up to its in-built standards, that we at least approach a condition in which all the people are independent and equal participants.

Of course, this is a wild idealization. No modern nation really lives up integrally to this standard. And many people have concluded that the inequalities in contemporary societies are so great as to disqualify them as genuine democracies. Others judge them to be, although very imperfect, close enough to deserve the name. I do not want to enter into this discussion here. I just want to draw out the way in which this standard generates demands for mutual recognition between groups.

The members of a sovereign people must be equal. But the demand for equality can easily slip over into one for uniformity. Indeed, this is what has been happening in Canada, as I will argue below, but here I just want to note that a sense of equality is a lot easier to maintain where the people are homogeneous. For once the people are rather obviously composed of two distinct groups – be it on racial, cultural, religious, or other grounds – a question cannot but arise. One group will be larger or more powerful than the other. In some ways the outcome of policy cannot but reflect this. But does this represent inequality?

To see what is involved here, let us look more closely at what we mean by equality in this context. It means something like everybody having an equal voice in the decision and everybody being listened to, even though in the end the policy adopted will be that of a majority only. We can see why homogeneity is an advantage. For where the people are a composite of two identifiable groups, the minority can ask themselves whether the majority are really listening. Perhaps the majority are working out their decisions, maybe even unconsciously, exclusively in terms that make sense to their group, or appeal to their interests and aspirations, oblivious or unmoved by the considerations that weigh with the minority. In this case, the latter will not be getting an equal hearing. They will be shut out. This means that the foundation understanding of liberal democracy will be violated in their case. The logic of the situation requires that the minority demand redress; or, failing this, that they strive to hive off and form their own sovereign people, capable within themselves of forming a society of autonomous, equal participants.

We have seen this scenario played out countless times in our world in the last couple of centuries, and we may be seeing it replayed soon right here. I make no claim for the validity of the judgments of equality or inequality in any particular case. I just want to show how this aspect of modern nationalism is not only a kind of inexplicable failing or irrationality to which some contemporary groups are prone (though it certainly can contain lots of irrationality). It is also a reaction that tends to be generated by the foundation demands of modern democratic society, and to deal with it adequately we have to understand it as such and not dismiss it as an aberration or condescend to it as a perhaps pardonable immaturity.

Generally, there is a sense of this in modern pluralist societies, and attempts are made to establish a common understanding around the principle of equal hearing. This can be done by entrenching the rights of certain groups. Canada has gone this route with the 1982 Charter of Rights and Freedoms, which establishes certain rights for official language minorities and, in another way, guarantees gender equality, and rights for aboriginals. These measures have an obvious place, because the most obvious denial of equality is actual discrimination against a minority, or its relegation to a lesser capacity in public life. So the struggle to maintain the standards of equal membership has often been played out in what one could call the politics of anti-discrimination. The most memorable case on our continent in recent decades has been the U.S. civil rights movement.

But even where obvious modes of discrimination have been neutralized, the issue of recognition can still arise. I am once more using the word in the modern sense, as correlative to the term "identity." Our identity is what defines us as human agents; it is "who" we are. The recognition I am talking about here is the acceptance of ourselves by others in our identity. We may be "recognized" in other senses – for example, as equal citizens, or rights bearers, or as being entitled to this or that service – and still be unrecognized in our identity. In other words, what is important to us in defining who we are may be quite unacknowledged, may even be condemned in the public life of our society, even though all our citizen rights are firmly guaranteed.

When this kind of denial takes place, or seems to do so in the eyes of a minority group, it is hard and sometimes impossible for the members of that minority group to feel that they are really being given an equal hearing; for what they stand for seems to be at best invisible and perhaps actively rejected by the majority, and thus cannot count with them. In effect, what pertains to the minority identity is not being given a hearing. In this way, a prolonged refusal of recognition between groups in a society can erode the common understanding of equal participation on which a functioning liberal democracy crucially depends. Canada is a tragic case in point.

In the above discussion, the situation of French Canadians in Canada has clearly been in my mind. But this is far from being the only way that the politics of recognition impact upon Canada. In recent decades, the West has in its own way had a sense of being a minority whose specificity has been unrecognized by the majority and whose voice was discounted. It is clear why aboriginal groups have felt themselves to be in this predicament too. At the same time, women's groups have been fighting for recognition of a women's agenda, which they see as being historically marginalized. Other groups as well have striven for redress.

The very number of such demands, and the way they lie athwart each other, make for a political scene of bewildering complexity. It can seem to make the objective of giving everyone a fair hearing impossible. We are coming close to the reasons for our impending breakup. The agenda of recognition is very differently framed in different cases. For some (French Canadians, latterly Quebeckers, and also aboriginals) the recognition they seek is of societies. For others (for example, women) the demand is to recognize a category of citizens with a particular life-situation. For others again, it is a matter of giving due weight to the people of a region. The very terms in which the issue is put change from case to case. By insisting that its terms are the only valid ones, one group can render invisible or illegitimate the demands that are vital to another. To refer to the well-known arguments rehearsed during the debate on the Meech Lake Accord, if you take the premise that the imbalance from which women suffer can best be righted through a charter of individual rights and if you want to make this the exclusive legitimate focus of reform, then you delegitimate the demand to recognize a distinct society.

It is all too easy to paint the agendas of different groups as incompatible and to pit them against one another as mortal enemies. We seem to have an almost fatal penchant for entering this path in Canada. Yet there seems to be something ultimately unjustifiable and absurd in this mutual exclusion. After all, what is the moral background that people appeal to in demanding recognition? It is some sense of a universal principle that everyone should be recognized. How then can people so easily define their demands so as to exclude others? Why are these demands so readily accepted by a wider public?

The answer is that the demand for recognition tends to hide itself, tends to be represented as something else. This is a major feature of the politics of recognition in our world. It is all the more difficult to work out in that it constantly transposes the terms in which it is couched. It is rare that a group will frame its demand as one for recognition in the sense that I am using the term here, that is, as a demand that such people be acknowledged and valued for what they are. It is much more likely to be put in terms of some injustice, discrimination, or systematic inequality that cries out for redress. Even where the importance of recognition for human beings is admitted, the language tends to speak of exploitation, power, even violence.

Thus, both feminist and black writers have spoken of the negative effects that belittling images of women or Afro-Americans have on the people so portrayed. When these images are interiorized, they lead to self-depreciation, even self-hatred; they induce passivity, demobilization. This is a way of acknowledging the crucial importance of recognition in human life. But its absence is portrayed as an act of aggression or domination, so that the accent is displaced from the human need itself to the interhuman drama of power and exploitation. Recognition withheld is portrayed as another act of discrimination, even violence, and can be treated in these terms. The issue can be dealt with as one of justice denied, rather than as a lack of openness to human diversity or an inability to discern the humanity of the other.

Why is there this displacement? It is not easy to understand. Partly it is that in making the simple demand for recognition, we cast ourselves as vulnerable; both pride and strategic considerations can make us reluctant to do this in a political context. It is also partly because the language of rights and injustice, of combatting discrimination, already has such a power and legitimacy in our world. It is something we want to latch onto in order to give our case force. These two motives intertwine. At the moment when one feels the need for recognition, there is always some question, some doubt, some concern about one's own worth. We can be seized by hesitation; we can easily waver. But once we can cast our demand in terms of justice denied, of rights withheld, then – damn it! – we have a duty to step forward and require that there be redress.

The transfer from a frank politics of recognition to a politics of antidiscrimination is all the easier where there have historically been inequalities and injustices. This is, of course, the case with French Canadians. And, with aboriginals, the injustices are not just historical but, in many cases, are continuing. The demand for recognition goes forward spearheaded, as it were, by a powerful sense of both historical and continuing grievance, the memory of which disarms opposition.

All this makes it hard to see what is going on. In spite of the continuing importance of real discrimination, a lot of the battle in Canada's present constitutional imbroglio is really over recognition. But the parties very often have the greatest difficulty being frank about this. Take Québécois independentism. The case for independence can be made *grosso modo* in three ways. One can distinguish three discourses. One is about powers: the jurisdictions that Quebec actually needs in order to preserve and promote the distinct society. Independentists claim that these include the full panoply of sovereign powers. A second is about dangers: the threats posed to Quebec within the existing federal structures, the chances that pan-Canadian majority power could be used to restrict the development of Quebec society. The third is about recognition.

The remarkable thing is that the third barely figures at all in independentist argumentation. The rational case is made in terms of the first two. But the issue of recognition is powerfully present in the rhetoric, where words like "pride" and "humiliation" have a big place, along with "acceptance" and "rejection." The sometimes embarrassing weakness of the arguments on instrumental grounds for more powers is more than compensated for by the force of the rhetoric of recognition denied. The aftermath to the rejection of Meech richly illustrates this.

This self-occlusion of the politics of recognition plays a very negative role. It makes it all the harder to bring things to a resolution. In the first place, others actually mistake what you are about. Once again, Meech tragically illustrates this. In Meech, the nationalist Québécois felt bound by their own strategy of occlusion to say that the "distinct society" clause was "just symbolic," therefore unimportant; and their denser compatriots in the rest of the country took them at their word and rejected it. But of course, the people who had decried Meech as "just symbolic" have been using the rhetoric of humiliation ever since to lever Quebec out of Canada. Anyone who can use the expression "*just* symbolic" has missed something essential about the nature of modern society.

This self-occlusion also makes possible the untroubled exclusion of the other I mentioned above. A demand for recognition clearly ought to be generalized to others. But if what we suffer from is some unique injustice that cries out for redress, then the other's agenda, which is merely about recognition, cannot be put on the same footing. This self-serving tunnel vision constantly threatens to lead the politics of recognition to an impasse.

I would now like to explore briefly the Canadian forms of this impasse as they have developed in recent years. Different groups in Canada translate their search for recognition into a concept of equal justice, which they then seek to set in concrete, regardless of the consequences for others. A wide coalition, including those who pressed for a policy of multiculturalism, some women's groups, and others, saw the answer to their aspirations in a Canadian Charter of Rights, conceived as guaranteeing equality between individuals. This may be a good solution for certain categories of citizens who seek recognition as such; but for minorities who define themselves as historic societies and want this acknowledged, it cannot serve. If the principle of the equality of individuals is taken as ruling out such a recognition of distinct societies, then in effect the answer to the aspirations of some groups is being defined so as to exclude others – in this case, Québécois and aboriginals. We are at an impasse. In a similar way, the sense of regional alienation has been translated into a concept of justice that entails equality between provinces. This is then taken as incompatible with a recognition of a distinct society.

These various forms of tunnel vision involve casting the whole country in the mould defined by one's own major concern, no matter how well or ill it fits others. Quebec has not been innocent of this in the past. The famous formula of the "two nations" fitted very well Quebec's own sense of itself as a nation, but involved projecting the same kind of unity onto "English" Canada, where it never really applied and has become steadily less apposite over the decades. The particularly virulent forms of this narrowness today get their strength from a moralization of politics: I impose my grid on society because it alone corresponds to true justice and equality. The high moral tone of this constitutional tartufferie is almost as hard to bear as its destructive consequences.

We might be able to strengthen the forces of realism and humility in this country if we could admit more openly that we are engaging in the politics of recognition. I am not claiming, of course, that this is all that is at stake in the present constitutional negotiations. There are grievances of many other kinds, other kinds of deprivations and injustices. And the demands include real transfers of power, such as those that would be involved in aboriginal self-government. But I believe that the real heat is generated from the perception of recognition denied, the sense that one's group counts for nothing or for too little. I think that it is this sense of grievance which more than anything else is bringing Canada to the edge of breakup; more particularly, it is the fact that the demands for recognition, defined so as to exclude one another, are making resolution close to impossible.

Here, the very success and prosperity of our country seems to play against us, as I hinted above. It is partly that the absence of other major crises brings recognition issues to the top of the agenda; and partly that the very success of Quebec society in recent decades has made the option of independence less fearful than it once was. But this also means that of the three discourses of nationalism I mentioned above – those of powers needed, dangers threatened, and recognition denied – it is really only the third that still has force. To the extent that Quebec independentism is still an *idée-force*, this is what gives it strength.

It was not always so. When Louis Riel was hanged, when conscription was imposed in 1917, the sense of danger, of being at the mercy of a potentially hostile majority, was uppermost. It is the very success of Quebec in building a state and a society which makes these fears seem obsolete. Quebec nationalism is full of fears, in particular for the language, and in certain ultranationalist milieux a dark sense of the threats to survival is *de rigueur*, under pain of suspected treason. But it is hard to generate a widespread sense in Quebec today that Canada is a threat. The real fuel for independentism is now elsewhere, in the discourse of recognition.

Indeed, a Quebec independentist might be defined as one who has utterly given up on seeking recognition from the Canadian partner and hopes to find this in escaping from the comparative invisibility of provincehood and moving into the international arena. This is why Quebec nationalists care so passionately how their society is seen abroad, and particularly in the United States. This is why a Mordecai Richler who presents an unflattering portrait of our language legislation in the *New Yorker* is seen as a mortal enemy of Quebec.

But this also means that the dialectic of misunderstanding between the two great societies in Canada has intensified. The reactions of each fuel the sense of rejection in the other. A Quebec independentist is one who has given up on "English" Canada as a recognition partner. This means that it becomes *de rigueur* for Quebec nationalists to affect a total disinterest in "English" Canada. It seems to be a matter of pride in some Quebec intellectual circles that one is totally ignorant of the cultural life of Toronto or Vancouver while expressing a lively interest in what is going on in Warsaw or Bogotà. This has been happening exactly in the decades during which "English" Canada has begun to awaken to Quebec, when Toronto writers, for instance, eagerly read and translated what was written here. Overtures were made, and were met with silence and indifference. The long overdue backlash is now upon us. Quebec no longer has *la cote d'amour* among the intelligentsia of English-speaking Canada.

It is not only among intellectuals that relations are soured. This by itself would not put the country in danger. There is a more widespread sense in the rest of the country that Quebec already has one foot out of the federation, that it is barely interested in continuing. So why tie oneself in knots to keep it if it really wants to go?

Seen from inside Quebec, it is not so clear that we want to go. But we broadcast very effectively the impression that we do, or else that we can only be kept inside by certain economic advantages. We somehow manage to obscure the fact that recognition matters to us, even while we make demands (such as the "distinct society" clause) which aim at precisely this. Our reaction to recognition denied is to pretend to the outside world that what really matters is something else, like the division of powers. We displace the issue and come up with documents such as the Allaire Report. This should not fool anyone, particularly when one sees how traumatic the rejection of the Meech Lake Accord was, how it reversed almost overnight a decade-long decline in support for independence. It should be evident that the studied indifference to "English" Canada is not a sign that recognition doesn't matter. On the contrary, it is a fruit of recognition denied. In the case of many Quebeckers, the turnoff is now irreversible; but for the majority it is perhaps not yet too late.

Yet growing numbers of Canadians outside Quebec manage to miss all this. They take us at our face value. (Here I mean our external face; because, if you live inside Quebec and listen, for instance, to what Lucien Bouchard can do with the "humiliation" of Meech, you find it hard to believe the indifference story.) Our two societies seem fated to miscue each other into wrong moves. The denial of recognition leads to the counter-denial that it was ever asked for, and to a statement of disaffection from the common enterprise; which is then met in the rest of the country with a sense of betrayal, even less willingness to recognize, and so on around again – unless the forces of realism and good sense can intervene in time.

Just suppose that they could, how could we live together in some kind of harmony? Let me finish this brief discussion by dreaming in colours for a few paragraphs. One way of framing our problem is to return to what I was saying earlier about the nature of modern democratic societies founded on popular sovereignty. A democratic society requires a certain kind of unity, because its people supposedly form a unit of collective decision. The various geographical components of, say, the Austro-Hungarian Empire in its heyday could largely ignore one another because they were held together only by rule from the top. But a democratic society is one in which people are called on to decide their common fate together. They have to be able to trust one another and have a sense of commitment to one another, or the whole process of common decision will be poisoned by division and mutual suspicion.

In other words, a democratic society needs a sense of common citizenship, that is, a common understanding of what it is to be a member of this society, which must include the dimension I dealt with above: the equality and autonomy of all citizens. That is why the modern democratic state generated something like a national identity – in, for instance, the United States and France – before the process began to be reversed and (linguistic) national identities began to demand statehood. That is why Canadians have felt the need to seek a national identity as a condition for the survival and flourishing of Canadian political society.

There is nothing wrong with this enterprise. On the contrary, in some form it is indispensable. But we have been looking in the wrong place, basing ourselves on the wrong models. One very prestigious model is that pioneered by the two earliest nations I just mentioned, the United States and France. To be a citizen of a democratic society is to be an individual with certain rights and duties among other individuals equally endowed. The citizen also belongs to other communities, familial, religious, ideological, built on tradition or affinity. But that is a matter for the private sphere. The state deals only with individuals, to which it accords rights and on which it makes claims. The state is a jealous community and can brook none other before it on a level with it.

A second model is now coming to the fore, partly because it is one that could have some importance in the definition of a new European citizenship. On this, citizens would belong to the larger entity via their membership in constituent societies. One would be a European through being a Frenchman, or a Spaniard. The superstate here would not deal with individuals as such but would recognize subcommunities.

Both these models are clear and easy to understand. The trouble is that neither of them will work in Canada, because both are meant to apply to everybody in the society. Suppose that we all belong to France, say, as individuals; then we might also all belong to a future Europe, perhaps, via our membership in national societies. But in Canada the problem is that different people relate to different models.

There are certainly masses of Canadians who understand themselves in terms of the first model. In the ten years of the Charter's existence, there has been an extraordinary growth of "Charter patriotism," the sense that this schedule of rights binds all Canadians together as equal individuals, regardless of their religious, ethnic, linguistic, or traditional ties. The point has been repeatedly made that the Charter contains more than a schedule of individual rights – that it also protects certain collective goals – but this is not necessarily relevant to its role in defining a citizenship to which many Canadians are glad to adhere.

By contrast, other Canadians – Quebeckers, francophones in general, and aboriginal communities – see themselves as fitting into the larger society (where they still do fit) through their membership in their historical communities. French Canadians over the last century have been members of the broader Canadian society through being members of *la nation canadienne-française.* That is why they often proposed something like the second model in talking about a Canada made up of "two nations." But this formula did not wash, because it involved imposing an alien mould on those who were not French Canadian. And it should be clear that the French-American model cannot work because it would involve imposing on Quebec – and, in another way, on aboriginals[2] – a formula that they cannot accept. Quebec is not just the home of some six million plus Canadian citizens, most of whom happen to speak French; Quebec sees and understands itself as a society with an aspiration to survive and flourish in its distinctness.

So what do we do? One answer is to give up. There is an alliance of Meech rejecters and Quebec independentists who agree philosophically on the American-French model. Both want tight, uniform, nineteenth-century nations; and both agree that this enterprise has to be carried out separately, by each society on its own. The other path would be to innovate. Suppose that we lived in a country where the common understanding was that there was more than one formula for citizenship and where we could live with the fact that different people related to different formulae. Suppose that we wanted to preserve our common political values, our mode of liberal democracy, and our ways of providing for our common needs – which in fields such as medical care are so different from those of our immediate neighbours. Supposing that we saw that we could best preserve these together, we might even allow ourselves to see that what is specific to each component – yes, even the French language in Quebec – can more effectively be defended within a broader Canadian frame. And we might come to be not dismayed and threatened, but even stimulated and enlarged by the differences we would have to bridge to keep this larger frame.

Is this such a crazy and offbeat idea? Perhaps it is the French-American model that is out of step with this age, in which international migration is rendering all societies more and more widely diverse and in which the politics of recognition is taking a larger and larger place. Perhaps the uniform citizenship society is the real utopia of the twenty-first century, and we can only live in as yet unexplored modes of deep diversity. A term such as "distinct society" belongs to this new exploration because it allows for difference. The first reaction of some people to this is to try to generalize it. Let us say that everybody belongs to a distinct society. (Hurry! declare everybody uniform again!) But the whole point of "distinct society," its advantage over the older demands for "two nations," is that it allows one group to breathe without imposing its model on the other.

What might a Canada that survived this crisis look like? It would unquestionably be dual in one important respect. There would be two major societies, each defined by its own dominant language. But each of these societies within itself would be more and more diverse. First, each would be more and more ethnically varied and, in different ways, multicultural; second, each would have significant minorities of the other official language; third, each would contain aboriginal communities with substantial but varying degrees of self-government. Neither would be a tidy, uniform republic. Come to think of it, something of what I have just been saying will happen anyway. We have the choice of going this route of diversity alone and in mutual enmity, or going it together in some relation of mutual support.

The latter might not be the promised land, but it would continue to be the envy of the world. Where Moses missed his Canadian future through his speech impediment, we are in danger of throwing ours away through a thought impediment. We are too fluent in the language of universal principles and exclusion, and can only stammer the speech of deep diversity.

Notes

1 See Charles Taylor, *The Malaise of Modernity* (Toronto: Anansi, 1991), and "The Politics of Recognition," in *Modernity and the Politics of Recognition* (Princeton: Princeton University Press, 1992).
2 There is an important difference here, which I cannot do justice to in the present discussion but which needs to be aired because it will

certainly lead to difficulties farther down the road. One of the reasons why it really obfuscates things to use the same term (say, "distinct society") for both the aboriginal and the Quebec cases is that the model of society is very different. Quebec already is – and is further developing as – an immigrant society in which people of diverse origins and traditions converge on a French-speaking culture that will develop out of it without being identical to the historical culture of French Canada. By contrast, aboriginal societies will mainly be made up of descendants of their present members; they will not want to assimilate large numbers of outsiders, nor will they be able to.

This increases the range of formulae of belonging which Canada will have to incorporate within itself if we take the path of deep diversity; it is another case where we have to avoid imposing the formula of one group on others. For an interesting discussion of different formulae, see Simon Langlois, "Le Choc de deux sociétés globales," *Le Québec et la restructuration du Canada*, ed. Louis Balthazar, Guy Laforest, and Vincent Lemieux (Sillery: Septentrion, 1991).

Index